'Building on his scholarly reflections, Professor Dimov offers a refreshing, action-oriented take on the entrepreneurial process and its inherent tensions. To take the entrepreneurial journey requires neither genius nor good fortune, simply a new mindset in which judgment is paramount and the future is contingent upon actions. As such, Professor Dimov's book is a call to arms to embrace the entrepreneurial journey.'

Denis A. Grégoire, Associate Professor,
HEC Montréal, Canada

'Dimo Dimov's contributions to entrepreneurship scholarship have helped to fundamentally shape the ways we think about the field. *The Reflective Entrepreneur* is a fine crystallization of his academic investigations, offering a highly accessible intellectual canvas for understanding entrepreneurship. A potential contemporary classic, I cannot recommend it highly enough to any researcher, student or practitioner interested in the dilemmas and tensions at the heart of the entrepreneurial journey.'

Stratos Ramoglou, Associate Professor of Strategy
and Innovation, University of Southampton, UK

'A valuable text that gets to the heart of the entrepreneurial machine – the entrepreneur themselves – by dissecting the entrepreneurial self. A new and exciting addition to the literature for those studying entrepreneurship and inspiration for those who wish to develop their own entrepreneurial mind-set.'

Monique Boddington, Research Associate,
University of Cambridge, UK

The Reflective Entrepreneur

In a world where entrepreneurial success often seems deceptively accessible, it is not always clear what makes a person entrepreneurial. In this book, Dimo Dimov offers a reflective insight into the entrepreneurial journey, striking up a conversation about entrepreneurship in order to challenge and untangle existing preconceptions.

A discussion of challenges and tensions such as idea versus opportunity, genius versus lunatic, and skill versus luck forms the foundation of the book, while the second part offers actions and considerations which can help the reader to seek opportunities in a fractious environment. The final part of the text focuses on the collective spirit in entrepreneurship, arising from the interplay between participation and outcomes.

The author brings a succinct diversity to the field, making this book essential reading for undergraduate and postgraduate students on entrepreneurship courses, as well as scholars, researchers, and practitioners looking for a new perspective on entrepreneurship.

Dimo Dimov is Professor of Innovation and Entrepreneurship at the University of Bath, UK.

Routledge Focus on Business and Management

The fields of business and management have grown exponentially as areas of research and education. This growth presents challenges for readers trying to keep up with the latest important insights. Routledge Focus on Business and Management presents small books on big topics and how they intersect with the world of business.

Individually, each title in the series provides coverage of a key academic topic, whilst collectively, the series forms a comprehensive collection across the business disciplines.

For a complete list of titles in this series, please visit www.routledge.com/business/series/FBM

Understanding the Born Global Firm
Neri Karra

The Internet of Things and Business
Martin De Saulles

The Search for Entrepreneurship
Simon Bridge

Neurobusiness
Stephen Rhys Thomas

Auditing Teams
Dynamics and Efficiency
Mara Cameran, Angelo Ditillo and Angela Pettinicchio

The Reflective Entrepreneur
Dimo Dimov

The Reflective Entrepreneur

Dimo Dimov

Routledge
Taylor & Francis Group

LONDON AND NEW YORK

First published 2017
by Routledge
2 Park Square, Milton Park, Abingdon, Oxon OX14 4RN

and by Routledge
711 Third Avenue, New York, NY 10017

*Routledge is an imprint of the Taylor & Francis Group, an informa
business*

British Library Cataloguing-in-Publication Data
A catalogue record for this book is available from the British
Library

Library of Congress Cataloging-in-Publication Data
A catalog record for this book has been requested

ISBN: 978-0-415-78572-3 (hbk)
ISBN: 978-1-315-22810-5 (ebk)

Typeset in Times New Roman
by Apex CoVantage, LLC

To Y, for enabling my reflective self

Contents

x *Contents*

Figures

Tables

Preface

There is a lot of excitement about entrepreneurship. We associate it with the significant changes it brings – the new products, services, business models, organizational methods that change the way we live and open up yet new opportunities. Many of us see it as a platform for autonomy and personal expression, as a means for solving problems related to the long-term sustainability of our planet and societies, and as a source of recognition and financial success. Policy makers see it is an engine of economic development and job creation. The media loves it because it offers great stories of going from humble beginnings to amazing ends, of venturing ahead against all odds.

One consequence of this excitement is that demand for learning entrepreneurship has shot up. Countless books are published on how to become a successful entrepreneur. Enrolment in entrepreneurship courses at universities has soared. Entrepreneurship is now making its headway into the secondary-school curriculum. At the core of these endeavours lies a fundamental question of how to teach entrepreneurship. And as soon as this question is posed, many people – indeed, many successful entrepreneurs – would argue that it cannot be taught; it is something one is born with.

The difficulty of tackling this question lies in the fact that entrepreneurship can be seen at several levels. At a broadest level, in terms of ultimate achievement or end point, it involves organization of resources and the creation of a new venture – whether an independent firm or a separate initiative within an existing organization – and thus can be described in terms of what needs to be put in place for this to happen. We need people, marketing, operations, etc. This is epitomized in the notion of a business plan as precisely what it implies, a plan for building the business. The challenge here is that we have a form, but no substance. When we answer the question of how to become an entrepreneur in these terms, we simply describe what a successful venture looks like and the elements it needs to have. A reader would be nonplussed as to what to do or how to proceed.

At a middle level, in terms of how we get to the end point, entrepreneurship involves a series of actions, that is, what entrepreneurs do in the process of creating their ventures. They make decisions, meet and negotiate with people, manage and lead people, solve problems. Every entrepreneurial story is a long stream of actions, of things done, challenges faced and overcome. The challenge here is with the lessons that we can extract from this sequence of actions. We are unlikely to repeat it, to have to do the same actions and in the same sequence, for our own situations will be different, indeed unique. Thus, we can get a detailed description of a process, but no logic that can recreate it. Again, a reader or a student would be nonplussed as to how to apply the experiences and stories of others to his or her own situations.

At a micro level, in terms of what explains each action and its relationship to those that precede it or succeed it, entrepreneurship involves facing and dealing with specific situations, of overcoming problems. We have a purpose, that is, what we aim to do or achieve, a set of circumstances and available information – from these we have to construct a course of action. Dealing with the interplay of purpose, circumstances, and information becomes a question of mindset, of a way of thinking, of procedural logic that can be applied to different situations regardless of their content. It is a mindset that has to be applied repeatedly, for the results of our actions in one situation become part of the circumstances of the next. This repeated logic becomes the building block of the broader journey and its outcomes.

The problem of approaching this micro level is that it requires displacement or modification of the ways of thinking that are already there, developed through socialization, education, and work experience, as well as by current narratives in the media. In teaching entrepreneurship, I have always faced the challenge of dealing with current preconceptions about it, of putting people on the same page before letting them experience it. When people face entrepreneurial situations, they resort to seeing them in preconceived ways, which suggest how these situations should be approached or what should be done. When there are no obvious solutions, the easiest answer might be that their ideas are not worthwhile or that they themselves are not suited for this sort of thing.

I have found that entrepreneurship puts people out of their comfort zone, as the expectations that their preconceptions bring and the certainty they demand clash with the uncertainty and ambiguity of the situations they face. People are often lulled by the clarity, smoothness, and inevitability of the entrepreneurial stories they hear, and they may expect to get the same feeling when they have an idea of their own and seek to take it forward. Needless to say, no obvious path reveals itself. In this case, we need to question and dislodge the preconceptions rather than the person or idea.

I see this book as applying a new coat of paint, a new way of viewing and approaching entrepreneurial situations. The biggest enemy of new paint is . . . the old paint, particularly where it is flaky or peeling off. To put a coat of new paint, one first has to prepare the wall – scrape off the loose bits of old paint until we have a smooth, solid foundation. Without doing this, the new paint will not stand – it will start peeling off in no time, unfastened by the unstable foundation underneath. The old paint in this case consists of preconceptions about what it means to be an entrepreneur.

The purpose of this book is to start a conversation with you, the reader, about entrepreneurship and its journey. I presume that opening this book is driven by your interest in entrepreneurship and perhaps your bubbling entrepreneurial energy: desire to solve problems, to become an agent of social or economic change, or to leave your own creative mark on the world through your ideas or visions. This inspiration and energy can quickly turn into dejection as the lack of clear signal or a sense of direction can be paralyzing. Against the clarity and seeming inevitability of entrepreneurial success stories, you might easily conclude that (1) your idea is not good enough or (2) you do not have what it takes.

The main premise of the book is that this perceived difficulty is self-imposed. It reflects a mindset that makes entrepreneurship a matter of superior judgment, thereby pressing one to search for the right decision – a decision that can be somehow justified. But the concept of 'right' requires a bounded context within which something can be determined as correct or optimal. And because the boundaries are set by what we already know, only an extension of the past can be justified. Entrepreneurship therefore requires stepping out of the judgment system as we know it.

In the words of George Bernard Shaw, "The reasonable man adapts himself to the world; the unreasonable one persists in trying to adapt the world to himself. Therefore, all progress depends on the unreasonable man". If we have to be reasonable, entrepreneurship would not be done. To do it, we have to step into the realm of unreasonableness. But how to do this without descending into chaos?

Most living systems operate at the 'edge of chaos', the fertile region between order and disorder (Kauffman, 2008). Too far a step in either direction can take them to the stifling force of too much order or to the destructive force of too much disorder. How can we walk this fine yet invisible line?

There are no ready or clear answers, but I hope that the conversation this book initiates will engage your reflective side and thus help you develop your own sense and find your own balance in your actions ahead. The book's title mirrors Schon's (1983) classic work that places reflection at the core of effective practice.

The book is organized in three parts. The first part looks to identify the flakes in the old paint: those implicit preconceptions about entrepreneurship and the entrepreneurial journey that, upon further scrutiny, reveal three irreconcilable tensions. I have synthesized these tensions from my own extensive research on the topic as well as from countless discussions and conversations that can be inevitably traced to one of these tensions. These tensions cannot be resolved; they have to be endured. But what makes them hard to endure is that they are underpinned by a need to exercise judgment. Thus, the final chapter of the first part seeks to prepare the ground for how this need can be contained.

The second part identifies and discusses the elements of the new paint. It focuses on the areas in which current implicit assumptions or preconceptions about the entrepreneurial journey need to be supplanted. One relates to the nature of the future and how to approach it. Rather than being inevitable or necessary, the future is contingent, unfolding through an interplay between purpose and constraints. In this regard, approaching it is a matter of dealing with immediate problems and setting proximate milestones. As we do that, we have to deal with both internal and external pressures and considerations.

The third part prepares the new mindset for action by raising awareness of the broader playing field. It first brings in the analogy of sport with its positive interplay between participation and achievement. By this token, entrepreneurship operates as an ecosystem, in which participation is individual (i.e. driven by individual effort), but outcomes are ultimately collective (i.e. determined by social processes). The second chapter discusses success as a result of natural attrition rather than artificial selection. This poses the question of resourcing entrepreneurship as emergent development, operating in stages and based on milestones.

References

Kauffman, S.A. (2008). *Reinventing the sacred*. New York: Basic Books.
Schon, D.A. (1983). *The reflective practitioner*. New York: Basic Books.

Acknowledgements

My academic work has placed me at the intersection of two vibrant communities, entrepreneurship scholars and aspiring and practicing entrepreneurs. In its own spirt, this book is effectively a collective outcome: the ideas presented here would not have arisen without innumerable productive encounters over the past 5 years. Although my purpose of understanding the entrepreneurial process has remained unchanged all along, each encounter has offered a new thread to follow – an idea, paper, book, video, a question, or feedback – and each such pursuit has opened up new intellectual vistas. What they all have in common is that it is easy to imagine that, without any one of them, history would have taken a different path, not leading up to this book.

I would like to thank all who have helped shape my thinking – fellow scholars, colleagues, collaborators, editors, reviewers, students, entrepreneurs, friends, and family. I am particularly grateful to Terry Clague for proactively supporting the idea of the book, to Mike Sotirakos and Jake Ronay for providing feedback and encouragement to earlier drafts, and to my family for giving me the space and support for thinking and writing, and for putting up with my obliviousness.

Part I

Tensions of the entrepreneurial journey

The evolution of business and indeed of life is a story of branching out, of pushing outward. We are fascinated by the next big thing, the branch that opens up new value, the new venture that brings great returns or changes the way we live. Whereas in life this is a natural process, driven by random mutations and an inherent instinct to survive and procreate, in business this is not a natural process, but one fed by decisions of what to do and where to invest resources. Thus, ultimate outcomes can be traced to specific, forward-looking prior decisions. And, naturally, there is a tendency to explain these decisions as somehow prescient or optimal, in order to derive some rules for such decisions to be made again in the future, in other circumstances.

The very notion of optimality, however, requires an outward boundary within which to exercise judgment of what the best course of action is for what we want. The present represents such a boundary in that it can vindicate or discredit prior actions and choices. At the same, for present actions and choices such boundary is to be sought – but not found – in the future.

There is an asymmetry between what we do and what happens. This is because in reasoning what to do, we have to set boundaries within which to exercise reason. Without them, reasoning is impossible – indeed thinking about everything is not possible because the question 'what else?' never ends. We have to stop somewhere and acknowledge leaving other things unspecified. What actually happens, however, arises from events outside of our control, at least some of which would fall outside of the boundaries set for reasoning. It is these surprises, whether positive or negative, that mark and define the entrepreneurial journey.

Branching-out structures are very interesting. If you trace them backwards, no matter from which end point you start, you will always run back to the beginning. If you trace them forwards, however, you start from the beginning, but cannot really know which end point you will reach – it is down to deciding which fork to take at each junction.

The knowledge asymmetry between present and future represents a tension that cannot be resolved. This is the case because without acting now the future outcome – whatever it might be – will not come about or will come about differently. But if one seeks to justify action by reference to future outcomes, such justification is possible only for outcomes that fall squarely within the current boundaries of reason.

This fundamental tension reveals itself in three different ways, depending on the viewpoint into the entrepreneurial journey, that is, its content, its person, and its process. One viewpoint is that of the prospective entrepreneur, of you and me looking ahead inspired by an idea. The tension there is between idea and opportunity. Another viewpoint is that of an external observer – whether a friend, a potential investor, or potential partner – looking at us as prospective entrepreneurs, to make sense of our optimism and aspirations. The tension there is between genius and lunatic. Yet another viewpoint is to make sense of the journey as a whole and to draw lessons from the way it has unfolded. This is captured by the tension between skill and luck.

The following three chapters focus on each of these tensions. In the fourth chapter, I draw implications from these tensions by returning to the question of judgment, highlighting its limitations and tensions as a guide for entrepreneurial action.

1   Idea vs. opportunity

People come up with ideas but, as entrepreneurs, they pursue opportunities. They pitch ideas to others, and these can be shot down as not being good opportunities; or they can generate excitement as great opportunities. Ideas and opportunities thus seem to be the same thing – images of a future – yet they feel different. Every opportunity originates or can be described as an idea, but not every idea can be deemed an opportunity. If we come up with an idea, we immediately start wondering if it is an opportunity.

At a first glance, the dividing line between the two is some positive judgment, a sense that the imagined future is desirable and attainable. But in the likely face of divided opinions, whose judgment matters here? We may be filled with optimism, with a sense of confidence, yet others may be more sceptical or outright dismissive. When one judgment is pinned against another, which one is right cannot be determined by . . . yet another judgment. Each judgment is underpinned by a set of beliefs about the future and none of these can be ruled out as wrong. Frustratingly, both may be right.

With the fallibility of opinion as a dividing line between idea and opportunity, the line can be drawn by the undertaking of some action in the name of the idea, that is, stepping forward towards the imagined future. The best marker of our positive judgment is whether we are ready to do something about our idea. Simply talking about it does not change it; it remains an idea, its possibility remains intact. But doing something about the idea does: it affirms our confidence in it and puts its possibility to the test. Thus, the very action in the name of the idea turns the idea into opportunity at least momentarily. This action brings in new information that can be used to update the idea and, in turn, if new action is undertaken, the pursuit of opportunity continues. An opportunity is thus kept alive through the repeated cycle of ideas and actions. An idea is static, an opportunity dynamic.

This poses an interesting puzzle. On the one hand, opportunities are ideas that are acted upon. Indeed, if an idea is not acted upon, whether it is to be considered an opportunity or not can be the subject of infinite speculation and debate. On the other hand, to act upon an idea seems to require a judgment that the idea is an opportunity in the first place. Hence the chicken-and-egg question: which comes first, the opportunity or the action?

This is a fundamental tension of the entrepreneurial journey, one that keeps the journey going towards revealing whether an idea is an opportunity. The tension can be resolved in one of two ways. One either abandons the pursuit of the idea, in which case the idea ceases to be an opportunity contender. Or one can reach a state in which the idea can be considered realized, in which case it is clearly an opportunity. Because this process hinges upon an evolving judgment that is often made quickly, it is helpful to unpack its elements.

The content of an idea and the nature of an opportunity

Idea and opportunity both refer to some form of business venture, whether undertaken as an independent start-up, as a separate initiative within an established firm, or in the name of pursuing a wider social goal. For something to be a business venture, it needs to have three elements: (1) a product or a service; (2) customers, users, or consumers of that product; and (3) an infrastructure that sources, creates, and distributes the product or service. In this sense, the business venture is a system – a social structure – of interconnected elements, namely people and some productive assets, as shown in Figure 1.1.

The individual elements alone are not sufficient to define the structure; it is the relationships among them that do so. Indeed, the very terms we use to describe the structure are relational in nature, that is, defined only in reference to something else. Thus, a particular individual becomes a customer only when related to a particular product or service; or an employee only when contracted within the infrastructure that produces the product or service. Similarly, something becomes a product or service only when related to a particular customer or a production infrastructure.

The notion of structure is essential here as it highlights the fact that it needs to be put together, meaning its elements gathered and weaved into the particular relationships. Consider the analogy of a building: it is a physical

Figure 1.1 Elements of opportunity.

structure in which its individual elements (bricks, concrete, glass, etc.) are put together as to form functional relationships that comprise the entire structure: foundation, walls, windows, roof. In the same manner, the entrepreneur creates the venture by establishing the functional relationships that comprise production and consumption.

The analogy stretches further. Before it is built, a building exists only as a blueprint – an idea in the mind of the architect or formally drawn. This blueprint takes materials that are taken for granted and imagines or draws the functional relationships that can be created among them. Similarly, before a venture is put together, it exists only as an idea in the mind of the entrepreneur that imagines relationships among people and productive assets.

Therefore, idea and opportunity represent two different viewpoints of the venture in question: (1) from the present, as an imagined future, and (2) from the future, as a realized future. The actions undertaken by the entrepreneur intend to move the venture along a continuum from 100 per cent blueprint to 100 per cent actualized, with all the gradations in between. Initiating or continuing the movement rests on two judgments. The first is a question of *possibility*, that is whether the future can be transformed from imagined to realized. Is the product/service even possible to make or deliver? And, if yes, will someone buy it? The second is a question of *profitability*, that is whether the realized future will be financially viable. Indeed, the expectation of profit is the essence of entrepreneurship. Will the basic economic transaction of the venture be profitable? In other words, will the price paid for the product/service be higher than the costs associated with producing it? And (how fast) will the money to be invested into the production infrastructure be recuperated?

To move from the imagination to the realization of an idea requires resources. At the very least, these resources include the time and effort of the entrepreneur, but can also include the time and effort of others, in-kind contributions of services or equipment, and financial resource that can be used to acquire equipment or services. Because the deployment of resources means foregoing all of their alternative uses (and associated benefits), the decision to deploy them involves making a sacrifice of sorts. Without this sacrifice, there is no realization of the idea. But with the sacrifice, the realization is not certain nevertheless, as evident in the looming questions of possibility and profitability. There is thus inherent tension in trading the certainty of current value for the uncertainty of higher future value. This tension cannot be resolved, but only accepted and endured until the effort is abandoned or realized. It is in this sense that entrepreneurs bear uncertainty (Knight, 1921).

Accepting the tension is a sort of plunge, of diving into the unknown with the hope and expectation of surfacing in a better state. Poised at the edge and staring at the abyss of an unknown future, we summon the power of judgment to determine whether what lies ahead is an opportunity or folly. Opportunity means jump, folly means stay; but neither answer is definite. In fact, it draws a line under a complex array of elements and considerations.

Possibility and profitability

The question of possibility

Take the question of possibility. It can be unpacked at several levels. At the start, there is the distinction of third- and first-person perspectives (McMullen and Shepherd, 2006). The former is the question of general possibility, that is, is this sort of product/service possible to produce by anyone and are there any people or companies out there who – as potential customers – would find it appealing? The latter is a question of more specific possibility, as faced by us, the particular entrepreneur. Will we be able to make this product/service and will we be able to find those who would consume it? If our answer is affirmative to the former and negative to the latter, the next question that arises is whether we can bring in others who can make things possible and, if yes, at what cost and effort. The answers to these questions are speculative at best and thus a yes/no argument cannot be resolved but for the one side to prove the other wrong. The proof has to be done not by argument, but by deeds. The best way to convince someone that we can do something is to do it. Anything else leaves hanging the possibility of being wrong.

In the first instance, we have to convince ourselves that the possibility is real. This can be done on the basis of a mixture of confidence and hope, which can reveal themselves as a hunch or gut feeling. The former rests on experience and its relevance to the situation at hand. The latter represents a feeling that things will turn out well or that we will make productive use of whatever happens.

The matter of deeds brings in a third question that focuses on the most specific possibility of how it will all be done. This is assessed against what has already been achieved, generating a sense of what needs yet to be done. The more there is still to be done, and the more far-fetched it seems, the lower one's confidence. For instance, we are facing a blank sheet of paper and have a picture in our head that we aim to transfer on the paper. We mentally project the picture on the paper and see it there, a structure of connected elements. But actually putting it on the paper requires moving the pencil around the paper. As we begin to do so, the picture starts coming alive. As this happens, there is less and less of it to finish and thus increased confidence that we will get there. Of course, this presumes that the lines are coming out exactly as imagined. If they do not, we can abandon the effort in frustration or keep trying on new sheets of paper.

The same logic applies when the picture in our head is of a business venture, a set of interconnected elements. Except that, instead of drawing it on a blank sheet of paper, we have to construct it in real life, of live elements, that is real people and commitments, and this brings a host of complications. The product or service needs to become real. To produce it requires real infrastructure. And those who will consume it will be real people. Thus, this is not entirely down to our efforts – whether or not we keep practicing – but involves identifying, engaging, and committing other people, whether as customers, partners, or employees.

To add to this complexity, our efforts will take place in real time. This means that all those other actors to be weaved into the social structure go about their daily lives pursuing their own aspirations and being enticed by other social structures. Perhaps some will find our product much to their liking. But if they happen to commit elsewhere before we make contact with them, it becomes a problem of bad timing. In addition, unlike the drawing example in which each blank sheet represents the same starting point, as we keep practicing, everything else around us keeps moving and changing, which means that we always have a different starting point and face new circumstances.

It is clear that producing evidence is the best way to facilitate the judgment of whether our idea is possible to realize. In other words, to convince ourselves or someone else that we can realize our idea, we have to start realizing it. And this of course means deploying resources and thus making the very sacrifices that were to be informed by whether our idea is deemed possible. This suggests that, at the very first steps, the sacrifice is largely underpinned by hope. As Henry Bergson (1913) observes, hope brings an intense pleasure, whereby we shape the future to our liking. In this regard, the idea of the future is more appealing than the future itself, because there is certainty about the future when contained within the idea itself, and uncertainty about whether it will look like that outside of the idea. The first step, therefore, represents trading the purity of the idea for the messiness of the outside world. It is thus not surprising that hanging on to the pure idea is often very appealing.

Figure 1.2 summarizes the interplay that occurs over time – as an idea moves towards opportunity – between hope and intuition on the one hand and tangible evidence on the other, exemplified by new information and commitments by others.

The question of profitability

Now, let's turn to the question of profitability. Again, it can be unpacked at several levels. One is the level of individual economic exchange at which the price paid for a product/service is compared to the costs of producing

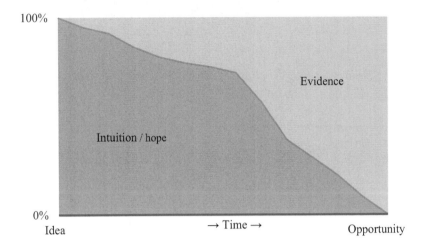

Figure 1.2 Interplay between idea and opportunity.

it. It is of course difficult to anticipate prices, but we can nevertheless use current levels for similar products to get a general sense. The matter of assessing costs is more complex. Without delving into the intricacies of accounting, it is helpful to distinguish direct and indirect costs (overheads). Put very simply, direct costs are those that can be attributed to the particular product and would not be otherwise incurred if the product were not made or sold. Overheads are costs that cannot be attributed to a particular product and are incurred regardless of whether the product is made or sold (e.g. rent or accounting office). They can be spread proportionally over each product sold; with more products, the overhead costs per product become lower.

With this in mind, profitability can be considered in terms of whether the price covers the direct costs (gross margin) and whether it covers the indirect costs (operating margin). The latter is dependent upon the scale of the business in the sense of over how many units the indirect costs can be spread. This leads to the second level of the profitability question, namely the scale of the business. As difficult as it might be to judge if any people would choose the product or service, it is more difficult to judge how many of them there would be. Indeed, history is full of examples where the scale potential is greatly underestimated: the first computer, Xerox's first photo-copier, the first Star Wars toys, to name just a few.

As well as being a cost driver, scale also determines the level of absolute profits that the business can accumulate over time. With increased scale, there naturally arise questions of competition and whether the scale can be maintained against its forces. The smell of profit is sure to attract competition and the easier it is for them to copy the product or service the more short-lived the venture will be.

Yet another level relates to the infrastructure that needs to be put in place before revenues start coming it. This is a question of upfront investment and of how it can be recuperated from the surplus generated from operations. It determines the payback period of the project, which can be estimated both in nominal terms (i.e. simply recovering the initial investment) and in terms of generating a return that covers the cost of capital, as determined by its alternative uses and level of risk.

It seems that the question of profitability can be posed and answered in terms of gross margin, operating margin, cumulative potential, or payback period. But what makes a level of profitability acceptable? This largely depends on the motivations of those looking at the venture and represents yet another level at which the profitability question can be posed. To be self-sustainable, a venture needs to earn its keep, that is, be operationally profitable but minimally so. Beyond such basic financial viability lies the matter of returns to the stakeholders involved, and these can be quite a diverse group.

Returns can be financial and thus assessed against competing investment possibilities. In other words, the venture is seen purely in terms of the financial capital that it brings back. Returns can also be strategic and thus assessed against the learning that venture produces and the possibilities that it opens up, such as the uses and benefits of a new technology. Returns can also be social and thus assessed in terms of the social impact that the venture will create, such as the alleviation of poverty or community cohesion. Returns can also be personal and thus assessed in terms of the inherent pleasure of being involved in the venture, for example in running a bookstore or a coffee shop.

Therefore, the question of whether a venture will be profitable calls for clarifying in what way profitability is to be assessed. Our own hunch for acting upon the idea reflects the specific mix of financial, strategic, social, and personal returns that we seek from the venture. But it is unlikely that someone else looking at the same idea would have the same mix of desired returns. Thus, when they make negative judgments, we have to view these against what they are looking to achieve from the venture or what they think that you are trying to achieve. It is not surprising that potential investors are rarely unanimous on whether a particular idea is an opportunity. We have to consider whether it is a question of not possible or not profitable and, if the latter, what kind of profitability is considered and what level is considered acceptable.

To recap the points made in this section, the tension between idea and opportunity is the driving force of the entrepreneurial journey. The journey is defined by the continuous resolution of that tension, reaching either a dead end or a successful realization of the idea. In this sense, idea and opportunity bookend the process, one marking its beginning and the other its end or realization. While they both have the same form – a social structure of production and exchange – they have different substance. The idea is a blueprint of that imagined future, while the opportunity is the actual relationships that comprise it. The movement from imagination to realization is mediated by the questions of possibility and profitability, the answer to which rests on a mixture of hope, evidence, and personal aspirations.

References

Bergson, H. (1913/2001). *Time and free will: An essay on the immediate data of consciousness* [Kindle version]. Mineola, NY: Dover Publications.

Knight, F. (1921). *Risk, uncertainty and profit*. Boston, MA: Houghton Mifflin.

McMullen, J.S. and Shepherd, D.A. (2006). 'Entrepreneurial action and the role of uncertainty in the theory of the entrepreneur'. *Academy of Management Review*, **31**, 131–152.

2 Genius vs. lunatic

The mixture of hope, evidence, and personal aspiration that drives the entrepreneurial process forward turns into prescience when the process reaches successful realization. Something interesting happens when the mere possible turns into actual: the cloud of uncertainty that surrounds the possible dissipates. It is in this sense that entrepreneurial opportunities are clear and obvious in retrospect, but opaque and ambiguous in prospect (Dimov, 2011).

What accounts for this asymmetry in perceptions is the passing of time, whereby multiple possibilities at every step of the way are continuously closed down with the making of history (what actually happens). When we look back, there are no past possibilities; when we look ahead, there are no future facts (Brumbaugh, 1966). In this regard, whether a vision of the future is a sign of genius or a lunatic dream can only be ascertained in retrospect.

During the entrepreneurial process, external stakeholders and observers play various important roles. They could be early confidants or sounding boards – friends or colleagues – who provide feedback on our thinking. They could also be investors looking to support the venture or journalists looking to cover it for the local or national media. In all cases, they form and offer opinions on the merits of the business idea. On the one hand, these opinions can be deemed objective in the sense that they are not coloured by hope or personal aspirations and thus only focus on the facts and evidence. On the other hand, these opinions are deprived from the very things that fuel the entrepreneurial process, namely hope and aspirations.

I have often offered a lukewarm response when asked to express an opinion on a business idea. Behind this lies a judgment that the idea has potential, but it is all a matter of execution. Indeed, I feel uneasy negating ideas outright, no matter how crazy they seem. My lukewarm response is sometimes assaulted by the hope and optimism of the entrepreneur who paints a bright picture of the future, of how things can work out for the better of many. I can't disagree with that or argue against it: even though there are no facts supporting the entrepreneur's optimistic position, there are also no facts supporting my own scepticism.

This is because there are, again, several layers of opinion involved. One is whether the picture itself of the future is great. We would readily agree. If the question, 'what do you think of my idea?' is rephrased as 'what do you think of the future I am aiming to build?', we would perhaps say, fantastic. There are of course times when we can question whether the proposed future is worth having. But granting acceptance of the end point, the other layer of the question is whether that future is feasible, that is, whether we think that the entrepreneur will pull it off. It interlaces the questions of possibility and profitability discussed in the previous chapter, but this time without the benefit of hopefulness or knowledge of what constitutes acceptable return.

As we contemplate these, we begin to imagine a stream of possible ways that the business can go wrong. It can get stuck on so many points along the way: the product/service may turn out tricky to make to the desired quality or at the necessary cost, people (customers) may not find it appealing enough, it may be difficult to attract talented people to the venture, the effort may run out of money, or there may be competing offerings whether by other startups or by existing companies who choose to respond to the threat offered by new players in the market. All these are evident hurdles, and it is not surprising that entrepreneurs are questioned on them in great detail by investors during a due diligence process.

These concerns are readily borne out by evidence on the reasons startups fail. Consider some of the top reasons mentioned: no market need, ran out of cash, not the right team, get outcompeted, pricing/cost issues, poor product, need/lack business model, poor marketing, ignore customers, product mis-timed, lose focus, disharmony of team/investors (CB Insights, 2016). These can be readily grouped into problems of market, product, finances, competition, and team. These problems cannot be tackled all at once, but step by step, with outcomes arising at each step of the way that would determine how to proceed next.

The point here is that what we have in front of us is a vast web of possible paths along which the venture can go, as illustrated in Figure 2.1. Many – or perhaps most – of these will lead to dead ends, while some can make it all the way through to some successful outcome. The complexity of the web depends on the number and complexity of tasks to be achieved: for example, the fitting out of a (coffee) shop, design and testing of a product, a long sales process with contacts, presentations, and negotiations. But standing at the outset and looking at this web of possibilities, we cannot know what the paths actually are beyond a few steps away, which path will transpire, or whether it will be a productive one.

Against the intimidating vastness of this web, we are to judge the optimism and confidence of the entrepreneur that she would navigate it through to a particular end point: it is difficult to be anything but sceptical. We can

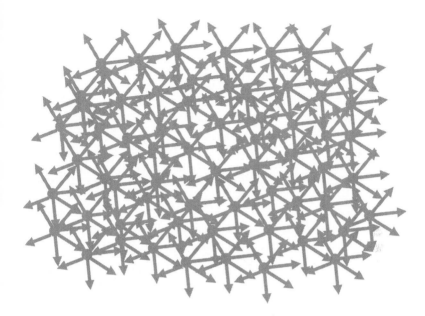

Figure 2.1 A view ahead of the entrepreneurial journey.

suppress the scepticism and turn it into encouragement, but it may quickly resurface if we are pressed to have 'skin in the game', that is, when we have to make a sacrifice in the form of money (as investors) or time (as advisors or team members). In these cases, what we wish we knew is whether the person standing in front of us is a genius or a lunatic. Whichever the case – but as long as we know it for sure – our choice will be easy as the decision to proceed or abstain will simply match the label.

Sorting out the genius and the lunatic

A logical way to attempt the judgment is to compare the person in front of us against successful entrepreneurs and see if they have matching qualities. This brings us to the inferences we make from entrepreneurial success stories. Against the web of possible paths and different ways in which that they could have not worked out, entrepreneurial successes are both impressive and inspiring. We feel a natural awe when we look at a successful person, which gives a glow to all their qualities. And why not? After all, all decisions and judgments made along the way, have turned out to be right in the end, even if not immediately. It is impossible to find the same type of glow in a person who is about to embark on an entrepreneurial journey.

The glow is in the eyes of the beholder. It can be traced to two sources. The first relates to the perception that there are no past possibilities. As history happens, all the untraced paths disappear from view; they represent alternative futures that did not come to be. The only thing that matters is the present as the future of the past. Against this perception, present outcomes seem clear and inevitable, in direct link to past junctions, as illustrated in Figure 2.2. In the words of the Nobel Prize winning psychologist Daniel Kahneman, "the illusion that we understand the past fosters overconfidence in our ability to predict the future" (2011: 218). As we treat the past as predictable, the only consistent trace all along – connecting the original idea with its successful realization – is . . . the entrepreneur.

The second source is the halo effect. It pertains to the tendency to judge the merits of a decision by the outcomes it produces (Rosenzweig, 2007). Every decision involves the weighing of positive and negative consequences. Such weighing is largely a subjective endeavour. Even if the probabilities of those consequences were to be estimated correctly, such probabilities would have meaning only in the context of repeated events or a pool of multiple events. For one-time events, they offer little guidance as a single draw can result in any of the possible outcomes. It is therefore difficult to appreciate the merits of a sound decision if ultimately it becomes marred by its negative consequences, even if those consequences had been acknowledged and considered. Similarly, a decision that is seemingly reckless can

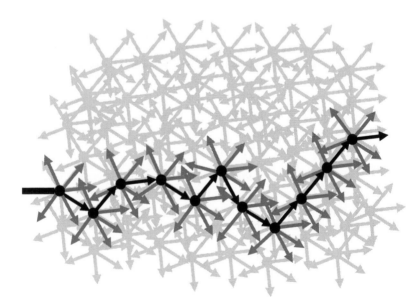

Figure 2.2 A view backward of the entrepreneurial journey.

be ultimately justified by the positive consequences it happens to produce. How can one argue that a successful entrepreneur had been reckless or perhaps taken a gamble that would be unwise for others to repeat?

Now consider how we look at someone who has been unsuccessful. There is no glow and no basis on which to consider prior decisions as sound. Against the difficulty of navigating the complex web of possible paths, we can feel respect at trying hard. But at the same time, the fervour and hope of the original vision now carry perhaps a hint of naivety (should have known better).

It is difficult to think that the difference between the two realizations may lie in a small and seemingly insignificant turn of events, but one that makes the paths ultimately divergent. Indeed, one hiccup can steer the entrepreneurial journey in an entirely different direction. For instance, a decision maker gone on holiday causing a sale to be delayed and ultimately to fall through as other events take over corporate attention.

A useful way to understand the entrepreneurial journey, therefore, is as a chain of events – each informing the next – whose effect is multiplicative rather than additive. The substantive difference between multiplicative and additive effects relates to the influence that a single event can have on the entire chain: in a multiplicative line-up, it can bring down the whole chain; in an additive, it can cause but a minor tremor. In other words, to succeed everything, needs to go right; to fail, only one thing needs to go wrong.

Consider the simple hypothetical example of a journey consisting of ten milestones (events), each with a 50 per cent likelihood of being reached. In this scenario, only 50 per cent of the entrepreneurs will go through the first step, 25 per cent through the second, 12.5 per cent through the third, and so on. Only 0.1 per cent will complete all 10 steps. Thus, from a population of 1,000 entrepreneurs, we are likely to see just one success, that is someone completing all 10 milestones. And, needless to say, he or she will attract a lot of attention, not least due to the admirable and improbable nature of their success. For the sake of illustrative comparison, there were approximately 9 million startups in the United States in 2015, equivalent to 0.31 per cent of the adult population or 750,000 starting a business every month (Kauffman Foundation, 2016), while only about 1,400 of them (0.02%) receive venture capital, that is, deemed to be high potential (PricewaterhouseCoopers, 2016), and still the majority of which will not deliver returns to their investors.

Sometimes nothing needs to go seemingly wrong in order for success not to materialize. This is because success is a matter of relative standing rather than absolute achievement, in the same way as it is in a sports tournament. In a close contest, few remember those coming second, no matter how close the result is. Think of a swimmer or runner winning by a tiny fraction of a second, a football team winning in a penalty shootout, a basketball team winning through a last-second shot, or a tennis player losing a fifth set 10–8 in a match that lasts close to 6 hours with several turnarounds. One single movement opens a discontinuous gap as it sorts the winner from the loser.

Looking forward rather than backward

Drawing inferences from observing winners leads to survival bias. In other words, we have no counterfactual against which to compare any characteristics we identify in the winners and determine that they indeed can account for their success. This is why it is difficult to draw lessons from a winner's account: any effort and any decision seem to contribute to the final outcome for it is easy to imagine that things would have turned out differently without them. The typical references to motivation, hard work, and persistence may ring true but they are likely insufficient to explain success. They are indeed necessary – without them there is no journey – but not sufficient.

What is more, motivation, hard work, and persistence represent qualitative states that will vary throughout the journey. Henry Bergson (1913) describes these as psychic states whose causes are within us and thus cannot be counted or even compared. At the most, we can talk about the intensity of psychic states – such as the intensity of feeling or of effort – but by admitting some degree of quantification, they become homogenous and thus lose some of their quality. How can we compare the motivations or efforts of two individuals, other than by reference to the tangible outcomes that they produce? When two people claim to be very motivated, work very hard, or be very confident, these labels make it difficult to tell the individuals apart. Language is an imperfect barometer.

How does that play out when looking at someone at the outset of their entrepreneurial journey, someone with a bold, but not yet realized vision? Without the glow arising from knowing that the person is a winner, we are likely to have different, perhaps mixed feelings. The boldness of the vision is appealing; the strength of conviction draws respect. But we can also see this playing out in many different ways. There are no future facts. Indeed, every proposition about the future has fractional truth to it, in the sense that it cannot be ruled out (Brumbaugh, 1966). Everybody is potentially both a genius and a lunatic! What is more, at the outset of the journey, we cannot judge how motivation, hard work, and persistence will play out throughout the journey.

While the journey will take place over time, at the present moment, we are standing outside the flow of time. There is thus a discontinuity between the present and the future in that the future does not exist other than as a vast range of possibilities. These possibilities multiply exponentially the further ahead we try to look, while the flow of time and the events and consequences it brings closes them down.

What is the flow of time? It is defined by the perception of change. We commonly equate it with physical time, represented by the standard units of seconds, minutes, hours, days that effectively represent external changes such as spatial positions or atomic vibrations. But this conception of time is not meaningful in the context of an entrepreneurial journey because the changes it represents are not relevant to the entrepreneurial purpose. The passing of time in an entrepreneurial journey is thus defined by the changes relevant to it, and this may bear little relationship to physical time.

In venture terms, the flow of time is defined by the milestones of the journey. A day can go by without anything happening on the venture front. In this case, venture time is slower than physical time. Or too many things can happen in a single day, in which case venture time is faster than physical time. When stuck on a particular milestone, we can get some sense of progress by breaking it down into smaller milestones, in the same way that we break down years into months, months into days, days into hours, hours into minutes, minutes into seconds. But unlike the physical time, milestones such as days, months, and years – which appear with predictable regularity, external to the journey and unrelated to our own efforts – the venture milestones are internal to the journey, affected both by our efforts and by the circumstances surrounding them. They are defined by whether the elements of the social structure that constitutes the entrepreneurial opportunity click together into place.

Each click can be seen as a binary outcome. It either happens or it does not: a customer makes a purchase, an employee or a client signs a contract, a product is ready for shipment, etc. The click is also a one-time event. This is because its situational circumstances are unique and also change with each attempt to bring it about. Thus, we are not really able to reset things and try again with a different approach, but have to work with whatever new outcomes and consequences arise in the meantime. Probabilistic thinking does not help in this situation.

The ultimate point here is that it is the flow of venture time that sorts out the genius from the lunatic. And yet, we seek to make this judgment outside of this flow, facing the next milestone. And while this milestone is looming, it is both there and not there; both options have an element of truth to them, yet neither is a fact. The only way to resolve this is to keep trying to reach the milestone (until doing so) . . . or to give up.

In summary, as we turn to others to promote our idea, we face the challenge of conveying what we see and feel to them. Our sense of possibility and hope are qualitative, intangible – stating that we see possibilities or feel hopeful convey little. Our fervour reflects the strength of our beliefs, but not their feasibility. Needless to say, we will see ourselves as but geniuses, yet with no tangible anchors others could easily see us as lunatics. When the external observer cannot distinguish the genius from the lunatic at the start, it seems that lunatic is the safer choice, particularly if judged by historical odds. Genius from the inside, lunatic from the outside: both have crazy ideas and aim to change the world. They both seem unreasonable against time yet to flow, against its overwhelming web of future contingencies.

References

Bergson, H. (1913/2001). *Time and free will: An essay on the immediate data of consciousness* [Kindle version]. Mineola, NY: Dover Publications.

Brumbaugh, R.S. (1966). 'Applied metaphysics: Truth and passing time'. *Review of Metaphysics*, **19**(4), 647–666.

CB Insights (2016). *The top 20 reasons startups fail*. Available at: www.cbinsights. com/research-reports/The-20-Reasons-Startups-Fail.pdf. Accessed on 3 January 2017.

Dimov, D. (2011). 'Grappling with the unbearable elusiveness of entrepreneurial opportunities'. *Entrepreneurship Theory and Practice*, **35**(1), 57–81.

Kahneman, D. (2011). *Thinking fast and slow*. London: Allen Lane.

Kauffman Foundation (2016). *Kauffman index of startup activity 2016*. Available at: www.kauffman.org/microsites/kauffman-index/reports/startup-activity. Accessed on 3 January 2017.

PricewaterhouseCoopers (2016). *MoneyTree report Q4 2015/full year 2015 summary*. Available at: www.pwc.com/us/en/technology/assets/pwc-moneytree-q4-2015-summary-fullyear.pdf. Accessed on 3 January 2017.

Rosenzweig, P. (2007). *The halo effect*. New York: Free Press.

3   Skill vs. luck

Are entrepreneurs successful because they are special, or special because they are successful?

When we face a successful entrepreneur, we are drawn to the sense that he or she has some unique abilities, to which we attribute his or her success and which we would like to find out. This is normal, a reflection of what psychologists refer to as the fundamental attribution error (Ross, 1977). When we look at great people, we tend to attribute their greatness to personal characteristics and downplay the situational influences to their success. Aside from these characteristics that we may seek to cultivate, we are also drawn to lessons or takeaways in terms of how to deal with certain challenges, perform certain tasks, or act in certain situations. Success stories are fascinating because they provide these answers in vivid detail, underpinned by the fact that decisions made along the way have paid off. Indeed, students in entrepreneurship classes consistently ask for practicing entrepreneurs to come to class and share their stories. They feel energized by the proximity of success and the sharing of its secrets.

One of the themes that consistently appears in these stories is the phrase 'I was lucky/fortunate': lucky to have met X; lucky to have run into X who told me about Y; lucky that when we talked to company X, they happened to be looking for a product like ours; fortunate that our first customer deal went smoothly; fortunate that the government had just initiated programme X, etc. These are usually fillers in between vivid descriptions of dealing with challenges or making difficult decisions. But perhaps they are essential to keep the story flowing. After all, if any of them had turned out differently, there might have been no story to tell at all. In terms of takeaways, however, they have little to offer us other than hope that things will play out favourably for us as well.

Drawing valid inferences from successful entrepreneurial endeavours is difficult due to the lack of counterfactuals. Entrepreneurs operate in different market, industry, geographical, and time contexts, work with different team members or advisors, engage with different customers. To isolate a particular characteristic or decision approach requires removing all this potential noise, which in turn is undermined by the lack of sufficient number of observations.

But there is a more fundamental point here about the nature of the null hypothesis in place – what we assume as the default explanation – from the rejection of which we draw our inferences. In the classic scientific inference, the null hypothesis normally presumes lack of systematic effect – that a particular outcome is down to random variations. This hypothesis serves as a baseline explanation, against which knowledge makes its inroads by an active quest to reject it. When the evidence is sufficient to reject this null hypothesis, then we can infer that particular causes are at play. But in the absence of such evidence, the null hypothesis remains the default explanation.

One might presume that a similar null-hypothesis logic applies to entrepreneurial success, meaning that in the absence of any evidence to the contrary, it is down to a random, fortunate constellation of events. This explanation would apply by default and we should actively seek to refute it by gathering evidence in a rigorous manner. But this does not seem to be the case. Instead, the opposite null hypothesis seems to apply, that is, that success is down to special abilities. How can you refute this in the case of a single, already realized entrepreneurial journey? As past possibilities fade away, it is difficult to imagine that things could have turned out differently. But even if we did imagine alternative paths, no reliable case can be made about where they would have led.

It is clear that our choice of default explanation affects the way we would react to a story of entrepreneurial success. Those who see success as a matter of special skills by default would see the vivid accounts as evidence for their default position. They would downplay the 'I was lucky' parts of the story as unreliable evidence that the story would have turned out differently. Alternatively, those who see success as a matter of fortunate constellation of events would see the 'I was lucky' parts of the story as undermining any claims to the contrary. They would question whether the vivid accounts imply anything special by arguing that the same approach could have worked out differently in different circumstances.

Accepting the role of luck in entrepreneurial success can be seen as a gateway to a more extreme position, namely that entrepreneurship itself is a random process, tantamount to pulling the lever of a slot machine. And since this is obviously not the case – there is clearly a place for focused, skilful effort, without which the process would get nowhere – it follows that luck should be downplayed. But there is a fault in this argument. It rests on the implicit assumption that seemingly random outcomes should necessarily arise from a random process. This assumption is not tenable: random outcomes can be generated by processes that are deterministic yet unpredictable (May, 1976). This makes recursive action – the continuous solving of arising problems – a powerful generative mechanism in entrepreneurship (Dimov, 2016). This has a number of important implications for understanding entrepreneurial success.

The nature of luck

What is luck? It refers to things that happen outside of our control and outside the realm of our reasoned action, and that have positive or negative consequences for our (entrepreneurial) efforts. For instance, we may choose to go for dinner at a particular restaurant, a decision that may have nothing to do with our entrepreneurial venture. But at the restaurant we meet a person who later becomes our business partner and, ultimately, plays a key role in the success of the venture. The original encounter at the restaurant was clearly a lucky one.

But in what way is it luck? First, perhaps we had no venture-related reason to go to this restaurant. Going there thus lied outside of our reasoned action for the venture: we happened to go there. Second, the other person happened to be there, but could have done a number of other things that evening (gone to the movies, stayed at home, gone to another restaurant, etc.). Her being there was entirely outside of our control. And even our very encounter was to a large degree outside of our control – we happened to be waiting at the bar at the same time and happened to be ready to strike a conversation, which happened to lead to our venture but could have easily taken a number of different turns. The most common word in this paragraph is 'happened'.

But this is not the first restaurant we have ever been to, and this is not the first person we have ever met and engaged in conversation. Yet, perhaps we (mostly) do not remember those other cases, but remember this particular one. Why? Because it has meant something for us down the line, it has led to positive consequences. Could we have known at the time where this encounter would lead and what it would mean? No. By the same token, the encounter could have had negative consequences: we would become partners, but he would be a difficult partner to work with, and we would get stuck in vigorous disagreements over the direction of the venture, contributing to its failure. In this case, we would probably consider ourselves unlucky with the encounter.

What this suggests is that events are not lucky or unlucky when they occur; they are neutral in the absence of any subsequent meaning. The luck label arises only retrospectively, when we can trace particular consequences to a particular event and when we appreciate that the event was not inevitable for a number of reasons. We can feel lucky at the time the event occurs, but just as the idea-versus-opportunity or genius-versus-lunatic judgments, this feeling can only be validated by some ultimate outcome.

One particular way in which luck plays out is in cases where we have done everything possible in a given situation, but its ultimate outcome depends on the deliberations of others. The classic example is our pitching to an investor or to a first major client, only to wait for the deliberation by an investment or executive committee. Despite the effort we have put into the presentation or the quality of the product, it alone cannot determine the outcome. The committees have their own interpersonal or political dynamics and their decisions can be hijacked by other factors such as the appearance of a rival alternative (another investment deal or service proposal), the absence of a key, friendly committee member, or the occurrence of an external event such as stock market crash or major bankruptcy.

Hence we hold our breath for a deal or contract to be signed or for a payment to come through. Regardless of how confident we feel, those outcomes can go either way as they are one-time occurrences. But without them, the journey stalls, the story cannot continue. And the longer they drag out, the higher the possibility that something unforeseen will derail them. How many entrepreneurs have gotten stuck on a deal that took too long to sign or a contract that has received various approvals through the hierarchy only to be stopped when, all of a sudden, a change of CEO was in the making?

Outcome patterns and the processes behind them

What do books and entrepreneurial ventures have in common? There are a few big hits and many, many moderate or poor performers. The vast majority of books will sell at best a few hundred copies, and only a tiny minority will sell in the millions. Seventy-six per cent of businesses in the United Kingdom do not employ anyone, 95 per cent employ less than 10 people, and only a tiny minority (0.1%) employ more than 250 people (Department for Business, Innovation and Skills, 2015). This performance pattern represents a long-tail distribution, as illustrated in Figure 3.1. The long-tail represents what would be seen as improbable outliers in a normal, bell-shaped distribution setting, but which are likely to occur and have a disproportionate effect.

The tiny minority of businesses (0.1%) employing more than 250 people account for 40 per cent of all employment in the United Kingdom and 53 per cent of all turnover. Long-tail distributions lie behind the well-known Pareto principle or 80/20 rule, stating that approximately 80 per cent of the effects come from 20 per cent of the causes. For instance, 20 per cent of the customers of a business provide 80 per cent of its revenue or bring 80 per cent of its problems. Such distributions are the norm in entrepreneurship, applying to its range of performance outcomes such as revenue, employment, and growth (Crawford et al., 2015). They are also prevalent in other

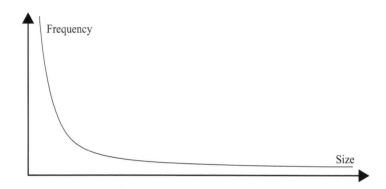

Figure 3.1 A long-tail distribution.

social settings such as music performance, movie performance, citations, size of cities, etc. (Andriani and McKelvey, 2009).

This pattern arises from two characteristics of the entrepreneurial task. First, it is a complex task, consisting of many sub-tasks and subject to chronological contingency. Second, it is a socially complex task, intertwined with the actions and preferences of other actors, which are in turn intertwined with the actions and preferences of other actors.

As a complex, chronologically contingent task, the entrepreneurial journey is a chain of events. Each event needs to occur favourably in order for the process to continue forward. In this sense, as discussed in the previous chapter, entrepreneurial outcomes represent multiplicative effects, that is, everything needs to go right; if one thing goes wrong then the process fails or changes direction. The more activities there are to be done, the more likely it is that any one of them might go wrong. When we consider that each of these intermediate events is subject to random influences – those that occur beyond control and the realm of reasoned action – then it is easy to see how the process is fragile in a forward-looking sense but appears inevitable in retrospect, when everything has turned out ok. More broadly, this resonates with the idea of normal or system accidents, whereby minor, chance factors can lead to major incidents in complex systems (Perrow, 1984).

The social complexity of the entrepreneurial process reflects the fact that success and failure ultimately depend on the commitment (or lack thereof) of others. Aside from the sales efforts of the entrepreneur, stakeholder commitments are socially interdependent: they depend on the opinions and decisions of others. This gives rise to social processes of diffusion and collective behaviour that have little to do with the entrepreneur but reflect the structure and processes of social networks in the transmission of information and preferences. There are two processes worth highlighting.

One such process is preferential attachment, also known as positive feedback and Matthew effect. It refers to situations where new customers make product adoption decisions on the basis of the adoption decisions of those before them. The more people like something, the more likely it is for others to like the same thing. Thus, more popular products become ever more popular. This process is difficult to foresee, as a few random choices of a particular product early on can sway future choices disproportionately in its favour. Facebook's early success is a prominent example here: what seemingly started as a leisurely activity was found cool by a few friends and eventually spread all over the Harvard campus and beyond, eventually taking a life of its own.

This process creates detachment between quality and success. An experiment by Salganik, Dodds and Watts (2006) involving the creation of an artificial music market clearly shows that when choice is influenced by observing the preferences of others, standalone quality has a very weak relationship with ultimate success. In the experiment, over 14,000 participants were given a list of unknown songs by unknown bands and invited to listed to any of the songs and, if they wish, download them. The participants were assigned to one of two conditions: independent, in which they had no information about the preferences of other participants, and social influence, in which they were given information about the number of times a song had been downloaded by previous participants. Moreover, there were eight versions of the social influence condition, each evolving independently. The results clearly show that social influence increases both inequality and unpredictability, that is, compared to the independent setting, in those settings (1) popular songs were more popular (and unpopular songs less popular) and (2) for a given quality, songs could experience a wide range of outcomes.

The second process relates to the diffusion of information and preferences and the differences in the mechanisms of contagion that drive the two, namely simple vs. complex contagion. In simple contagion, information is passed by one person to another by mere contact, whether personal or through the media. While this works for information, it does not work for preferences and choices. For many people, simply knowing about a product is insufficient to drive a decision to consume it. Their choices are determined by the choices of those around them (e.g. friends, family, colleagues, or professional peers); only when a sufficient proportion of those have made the same choice does the focal person decide to adopt the product. In this process of complex contagion, the structure of the social network matters and clusters of interconnected people become barriers to wider adoption (Easley and Kleinberg, 2010).

The nature of complex contagion is what lies at the heart of Moore's (1991) classic book about the challenges of marketing high-technology products to mainstream customers. By segmenting people on the basis of their attitude towards new product adoption, Moore identifies a 'chasm' in the qualitatively different ways in which 'early adopters' and 'early majority' make their adoption decision: the former are swayed by simply learning about new products (simple contagion), while the latter require evidence from the experience of their peers (complex contagion). The niche approach recommended by Moore – concentrating initial efforts on a small segment – reflects the fact that complex contagion requires more concentrated effort to win over a cluster. Indeed, many entrepreneurs speak of hoping to trigger an avalanche of product adoption, which reflects the cascade effect associated with breaking into a cluster.

In summary, the question of whether entrepreneurial success is a matter of skill or luck continues to inspire debate. In one sense, it is a matter of one's adoption of skill or luck as the default explanation. The former arises naturally from people's fundamental attribution error. The latter represents the natural scepticism of a scientifically minded observer.

Of course, the picture is more nuanced. It is not a matter of one or the other, but a matter of both. Entrepreneurship cannot be 100 per cent skill – think of all the outcomes beyond the entrepreneur's control that need to go right. And it cannot be 100 per cent luck – think of tasks that require some minimum level of skill. It is thus useful to think of a continuum ranging from 100 per cent skill to 100 per cent luck on which we can place the entrepreneurial journey in respect to its realization.

Mauboussin (2012) provides an insightful approach to doing so by decomposing the overall variance of outcomes into variance due to skill and variance due to luck. Based on extensive data on sports performance, he estimates the role of luck to be 12 per cent in basketball, 31–34 per cent in baseball, 38 per cent in American football, and 53 per cent in hockey. Applying the same logic to investing, he estimates the role of luck there at 80–85 per cent. Particularly relevant for appreciating the interplay between skill and luck is what he terms the 'paradox of skill': as skill improves and thus makes performance more consistent, luck increases its role in determining competitive outcomes.

In applying this logic to business activities, Mauboussin (2012) makes a useful distinction between (1) routine or repetitive tasks such as operations, for which the predictability of performance makes them conducive to the development of skill; and (2) non-routine tasks such as setting new strategy or venturing in new areas that require experimental approaches, for which the unpredictability of outcomes makes them susceptible to luck. Thus, we would expect the skill-luck mix to vary with a company's relative mix of these activities. In the entrepreneurial journey, the non-routine tasks dominate its early stages as the venture seeks a solid foundation, a viable business model. In its later stages, the routine tasks may become more prevalent as the venture gears up to scale and grow from an already established foundation. Therefore, we would expect the role of luck to be high at the beginning of the journey (perhaps as high as 80–85 per cent, as in the case of investing), but decline over time as more routine skills take over.

Where does this leave us? With the sense that skill is necessary but not sufficient. It is important to keep the process going towards the next milestone, but how the process ultimately plays out is perhaps a matter of luck. Entrepreneurship is thus tantamount to an art of surviving until we get lucky.

References

Andriani, P. and McKelvey, B. (2009). 'From Gaussian to Paretian thinking: Causes and implications of power laws in organizations'. *Organization Science*, **20**(6), 1–19.

Crawford, G.C., Aguinis, H., Lichtenstein, B., Davidsson, P. and McKelvey, B. (2015). 'Power law distributions in entrepreneurship: Implications for theory and research'. *Journal of Business Venturing*, **30**(5), 696–713.

Department for Business, Innovation and Skills (2015). *Business population estimates for the UK and regions 2015*. Available at: www.gov.uk/government/uploads/system/uploads/attachment_data/file/467443/bpe_2015_statistical_release.pdf. Accessed on 3 January 2017.

Dimov, D. (2016). 'Toward a design science of entrepreneurship'. In A.C. Corbett and J.A. Katz (Eds.), *Advances in entrepreneurship, firm emergence and growth*. Bingley, UK: Emerald Insight, Vol. 18, 1–31.

Easley, D. and Kleinberg, J. (2010). *Networks, crowds, and markets: Reasoning about a highly connected world*. Cambridge, UK: Cambridge University Press.

Mauboussin, M.J. (2012). *The success equation: Untangling skill and luck in business, sports, and investing*. Boston, MA: Harvard Business Review Press.

May, R.M. (1976). 'Simple mathematical models with very complicated dynamics'. *Nature*, **261**, 459–467.

Moore, G.A. (1991). *Crossing the chasm*. New York: Harper Business.

Perrow, C. (1984). *Normal accidents: Living with high-risk technologies*. New York: Basic Books.

Ross, L. (1977). 'The intuitive psychologist and his shortcomings: Distortions in the attribution process'. In L. Berkowitz (Ed.), *Advances in experimental social psychology*. New York: Academic Press, Vol. 10, 173–220.

Salganik, M.J., Dodds, P.S. and Watts, D.J. (2006). 'Experimental study of inequality and unpredictability in an artificial cultural market'. *Science*, **311**, 854–856.

4 Judgment and the entrepreneurial journey

The three tensions outlined in the previous chapters affirm the asymmetry between the future as anticipated from the present and the future as it happens or has happened. The former is an unbounded set of possibilities that keep opening the more we think about what may happen ahead. The latter is the closing down of these possibilities, their convergence into the actualities that comprise the path of history.

Both possibilities and actualities invite judgment, albeit of different nature. Possibilities invite immediate choice or justification, because only one path can be followed as the next step. When we step forward, it matters that what we do seems reasonable, that our course of action can be explained or justified. Unless we choose to act in an unreasonable manner, which nevertheless requires a sense of what is reasonable as a benchmark. This is a matter of normative assessment of a prospective action as right or wrong. But at the same time, what actually happens can also vindicate prior actions if the outcome it brings is beneficial. Thus, actualities invite qualitative evaluation of the action as good or bad in view of its consequences.

Information and action

Both justification and evaluation are structurally constrained in regard to their placement relative to an action and its consequences. Because there are no past possibilities, justification cannot be exercised after the action, when all the alternative possibilities have disappeared. And because there are no future facts, evaluation cannot be exercised before the action, when all its consequences have not yet appeared.

In addition, both justification and evaluation have inherent limitations related to the difference in the information available before and after the action. Because what actually happens is based on events, actions, and information that are not available at the time of any beforehand deliberation, those cannot be part of that deliberation. Therefore, to the extent that deliberation aims to anticipate and compare future outcomes for the purpose of justification, justification has a blindspot.

Similarly, because the consequences of what actually happens may be related to events that have little to do with the action itself – a pure time coincidence or externality – it is impossible to identify consequences that are uniquely attributable to these events and thus would not have occurred had a different set of events coincided with the action. Therefore, to the extent that such events are inevitably part of the evaluation exercise, evaluation has a blindspot. The two blindspots are illustrated in Figure 4.1.

Figure 4.1 also illustrates the interplay between the information sets available before and after the action in relation to the events and their consequences. As well as occurring for unrelated reasons, these events/consequences can be triggered by the very action we undertake, by inviting responses, reactions, and counteractions by those affected. Some of these may be genuinely unexpected, in a positive or negative sense. For instance, excitement about a new product may be much stronger than anticipated and some of the prospective customers may proactively decide to become active advocates of the product. Or prospective customers may identify uses of the product that are potentially harmful and thus require re-examination of its specification.

Others can be expected, in the sense of being able to anticipate the set of possible outcomes (e.g. a yes or no answer), but not being able to know which one of them will transpire. Until that outcome occurs, all its alternative realizations have to be considered possible and real. In this regard, prior to the action, deliberation is marred by the impossibility of focusing on only one of these possible outcomes, and thus the need to contain them all, each with its own tree of further possibilities. In contrast, after the action, there is clarity in terms of which outcome has transpired, thereby enabling us to focus on the new possibilities it opens up. In effect, the action cuts off all the branches of the tree of possibilities associated with the outcomes that did not occur. This is illustrated in Figure 4.2.

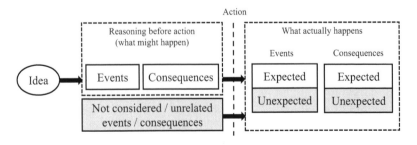

Figure 4.1 Blindspots in entrepreneurial judgment.

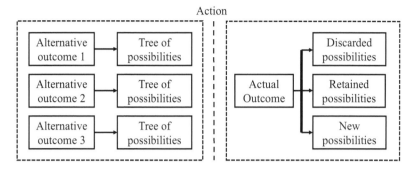

Figure 4.2 Consideration sets before and after action.

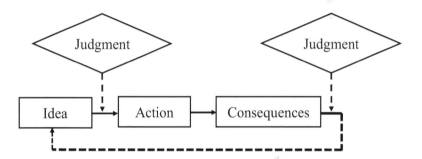

Figure 4.3 Two places for exercising judgment.

Judgment and action

In a general sense, judgment pertains to the evaluation of information to make a decision. It is a faculty to be exercised at the discretion of the decision maker and to serve a particular purpose. The entrepreneurial journey consists of many action points, each following the previous and setting up the next. Purpose evolves and, in each action situation, reveals itself as an immediate problem to solve, an idea of what we want to achieve at the next step.

In this regard, the set of idea, action and consequences represents a basic unit of the entrepreneurial journey that is repeated over and over again. The question then arises of where to place judgment within this unit. We can place judgment in two different time spots and thus exercise it in two different ways, as shown in Figure 4.3.

Judgment before action

We can exercise judgment between idea and action, as a means to justify or sanction a proposed action. It is based on the anticipation of the consequences of the action and, as such, is inherently limited by the information available prior to the action. Such judgment proclaims an action as right or wrong. It is used to rule out certain projects or actions on the basis that they do not have the right ideas, the right person, or the right skills.

This type of judgment represents a logic of pushing forward (De Bono, 1993). It operates a truth system, based on the question 'what is the right action?' and involves a comparison of the information at hand with the ideal generated by a truth system. This judgment operates with a threshold for weight of evidence, that is, the evidence provided in support of the action needs to be based on facts to a certain degree. This can be both an advantage and a limitation. The advantage is that it minimizes failure by eliminating speculative actions that can lead to dead ends. This reduces the costs of sacrifices. The limitation is that it undercuts successes at the same time, by precluding actions from getting lucky, lunatics from turning into geniuses, wild ideas from turning into opportunities.

If we think back to the original idea–opportunity continuum, which ranges from 100 per cent blueprint to 100 per cent actualized, it is clear that the closer we are to the blueprint end of the continuum the smaller the set of facts on which we can rely (Figure 1.2). At the outset of the entrepreneurial journey, when we have 100 per cent blueprint, the projected consequences are based on intuition and hope. Any attempt to exercise sound judgment is bound to raise a red flag for the action. This is the position in which many entrepreneurs find themselves, whether as part of start-up efforts or initiatives within existing organizations. They are asked to produce evidence that their actions will pay off. In the absence of tangible or reliable evidence, the action cannot be sanctioned.

While it is possible to overcome this hurdle by circumstantial evidence such as the track record of the entrepreneur or the track record of similar initiatives, the point here is that it is the need to exercise the judgment itself that creates the tension. Eliminating the judgment altogether removes accountability for the decision. At the same time, accountability is important in the light of the sacrifice that the decision brings, in terms of time, resources, or opportunity costs. The bigger the sacrifice, the stronger the need for accountability, and thus the stronger the pressure to exercise such prospective judgment.

Judgment after action

We can also exercise judgment after an action, as a means to evaluate its consequences. It makes full use of the information generated from the action to consider the new action possibilities that open up. Such a judgment proclaims an action as good or bad. While it does not rule out certain projects or actions at the outset, it subjects them to natural attrition, eliminating those that do not work out.

This type of judgment follows a logic of jumping ahead, that is, movement for the sake of identifying the possibilities it opens up, without being subject to justification (De Bono, 1993). It aims to formulate a promising next step, based on the learning and outcomes produced by the action. Again, this can be both an advantage and a limitation. The advantage is that it maximizes success by increasing exposure to serendipity. It is notable that entrepreneurial breakthroughs often come from such jumps as new possibilities open up in unanticipated ways. The limitation is that the costs of sacrifices need to be borne out and can easily become unaffordable if we let every action play out.

Therefore, judgment eliminates or narrows down action possibilities. This is done prospectively when judgment is exercised before an action, or retrospectively when it is exercised after an action. The two different options utilize different information sets. Transitioning between the two, we bear the uncertainty associated with bifurcated possibilities and experience the emergence of unanticipated events and their consequences. While the former judgment minimizes failure at the expense of success, the latter maximizes success at the expense of failure. Therefore, the urge to exercise the former needs to be restrained, while the indulgence of the latter needs to be contained.

Individual vs. collective perspectives

The locus of the exercised judgment introduces yet another tension, namely between the individual entrepreneur and the broader entrepreneurial community. From the point of view of the individual entrepreneur, what matters is whether they are successful or not. The success of others is not immediately relevant. This suggests that the desire to succeed can generate persistence and optimism way above what may be warranted in the given circumstances. But it may also trigger a focus on avoiding failure in a way that prevents more speculative moves.

The issue here arises when we stake our entrepreneurial journey on experiencing success and thus may start looking for the evidence of success before undertaking action. The typical example of this is when we look exclusively to make money and start evaluating ideas on this basis. Early on, the money-making potential of most ideas is not evident and hence they are discarded. A classic example of this is Intel's declining to fabricate the processor that would power the future iPhone on the grounds of insufficient forecast volume, which in retrospect underestimated the eventual demand by a factor of 100. The words of Intel's CEO at the time, Paul Otellini are telling: "This was before the iPhone was introduced and no one knew what the iPhone would do" (Madrigal, 2013: paragraph 9). The point here is not to blame the faulty forecasts (almost all forecasts for new products end up being faulty), but to recognize that the very reliance on forecasts to justify a decision makes it impossible to proceed with an idea at its early stages.

From a community point of view, however, what matters is that at least one entrepreneur is successful. It does not matter who. From this perspective, one would encourage a wide range of ideas and actions with the sense that this maximizes the likelihood of any one of them reaching success. In this sense, as a collective endeavour – each entrepreneur pursuing their own idea while also building upon and contributing to the ideas and efforts of others – entrepreneurship becomes much more powerful than the efforts of any single individual. Its range of exploration and experimentation is vastly larger. The challenge here is to contain the costs associated with enabling this large degree of experimentation.

Consider the example of a cohort of 100 potential entrepreneurs. If they all act to pursue their ideas, we can sit comfortably on the expectation that at least a few of the efforts will be successful. This squares with the long-tail distributions discussed in the previous chapter. It will create a good track record for the cohort overall. For the individual entrepreneurs, however, the sense that only one of them makes it can be a source of anxiety. They might wonder, 'will it be me? I want it to be me!' On the binary criterion of success/failure, most will be disappointed, while only a few will be happy with the outcome.

On the same criterion, the collective as a whole is happy. Can the disappointment of most be outweighed by the success of one? Yes, if the focus is on the non-commercial aspects of the entrepreneurial journey such as the pleasure of pursuing one's passion and the learning that the journey provides; or if the entrepreneurial spirit is collective in nature. This characterizes vibrant entrepreneurial ecosystems, permeated by a culture of inclusiveness, mentorship, mobility, and increasing returns (Feld, 2012).

Similar logic drives the economics of venture capital investing, where one success can compensate for many failures. But because it cannot be known at the outset which of the initial investments will be successful, it is necessary to invest in and nurture a larger portfolio. While investment theory regards portfolios as tools for diversification of risk – that is, for minimizing the risks for given levels of return – they can also operate as means for maximizing success.

Between order and disorder

In summary, judgment plays an important part in the entrepreneurial journey, revealing itself in seeking justification for an action or in evaluating its consequences. The first type of judgment deals with the question of whether it is worthwhile to pursue or persist with an idea. This is a question of *why* and it serves as a gatekeeper for action, an artificial sanctioning of it. In this judgment, the pursuit of the idea is put against alternative uses of our time and resources. To be answered in the affirmative, there need to be clear and compelling benefits. These benefits can be related to the process itself (e.g. experience, learning, the enjoyment of doing something you are passionate about) or to the outcomes it produces (e.g. financial wealth).

The second type is an evaluative judgment of the action as good or bad, based on the possibilities for further action and the development it opens up. This is a question of *where next*, and it offers a natural attrition for the action, meaning that at some point, it may reach a dead end. The benefits of the action can include valuable new information about preferences and consequences, new commitments or new resources.

Both judgments can serve as impediments to the entrepreneurial journey. If a specific benefit needs to be demonstrated beforehand, very few ideas will pass the sanctioning screen. Those screened out will certainly include the more radical, more speculative ones, yet with high potential nevertheless. Similarly, against specific expectations, the information produced by an action may not be deemed useful. Thus, when these judgments are exercised too tightly, the result is low sanction and high attrition. But equally, these judgments cannot be eliminated. In the absence of any steer, any effort becomes worthwhile. Similarly, against loose expectations, any action would be deemed good as the information it produces is bound to have some use. The result is high sanction and low attrition.

Therefore, the two judgments need to work in unison, capitalizing on the knowledge available both before and after the action and striking a balance between sanction and attrition. This resonates with the idea of 'edge of chaos' as a fertile zone in between order and disorder (Kauffman, 2008). The interplay between sanction and attrition is illustrated in Table 4.1.

The challenge for the journey is to keep it in this fertile zone, balancing its inherent tensions. The next section will explore the questions that underpin this challenge and derive from them a set of action principles that can help us take it on.

Table 4.1 Interplay between sanction and attrition

	Tight expectations		*Loose expectations*
Justification (Why?)	Low sanction		High sanction
		Edge of chaos	
Evaluation (Where next?)	High attrition		Low attrition

References

De Bono, E. (1993). *Teach your child how to think*. London: Penguin.
Feld, B. (2012). *Startup communities*. Hoboken, NJ: John Wiley & Sons.
Madrigal, A.C. (2013). 'Paul Otellini's Intel: Can the company that built the future survive it?' *The Atlantic*, 16 May 2013. Available at: www.theatlantic.com/technology/archive/2013/05/paul-otellinis-intel-can-the-company-that-built-the-future-survive-it/275825/. Accessed on 3 January 2017.

Part II

The journey from the inside

The previous section discussed three tensions that characterize the entrepreneurial journey, driven by the asymmetry between the imagined and realized future. This asymmetry creates blindspots for the two types of judgment – justification and evaluation – that arise in the journey in respect to the actions that comprise it. Both judgments can stifle the journey, yet neither can be dispensed with. Hence the challenge for this section – how to avoid succumbing to the temptations of each type of judgment and to keep the journey in the fertile zone between order and disorder.

How harshly the judgments are exercised is a matter of our mindset, whether as individuals or organizational decision makers. To what extent do we need to have a clear reason in order to do something? And to what extent should this reason be an identifiable future state? This reflects a fundamental predisposition towards the future that pushes our reasoning beyond the edge of time. We seek to run ahead of time, to check the future out before we approach it, to make it tangible in the present. This is a quest for certainty, without which becoming an entrepreneur feels like a plunge into the unknown. But unlike running ahead in the forest to check that the path is clear, the only running we do is within our head, and the only path we check is the one produced by the limitations of our imagination and reasoning.

As I will explore in Chapter 5, this attitude rests on implicit assumptions about the nature of the future and the way to approach it. The chapter will ask you to replace the notion of the future as arising out of necessity with the notion of the future as arising out of contingency. This is a vital switch. Just like the fundamental setting of an electronic device – a frequency switch or a language setting – it makes the previously inaccessible accessible.

Against a contingent future, I outline two basic action logics – (1) getting to the next milestone and (2) changing direction – each subject to internal and external pressures or considerations, giving rise to four sets of action principles. I explore these in the following chapters. In Chapter 6, I discuss the nature of the milestones in the entrepreneurial journey, and in Chapters 7 and 8, the internal and external pressures that bear upon the journey.

5 Future

The need to consider ultimate outcomes arises when the entrepreneurial journey is seen simply as a vehicle for delivering other benefits such as financial wealth or recognition. To attain those, it does not really matter what we do, as long as it leads to their attainment. Hence the question of why we seek to become entrepreneurs. Is it for the sake of what it involves or for the sake of what it brings? Even when organizations create specific jobs to focus on entrepreneurship or innovation, thereby eliminating the need to justify the behaviour of the people holding them, the focus on entrepreneurship in the first place is often driven by the need to deliver new revenues or sustain the bottom line over time.

Therefore, when entrepreneurship is appreciated for what it would bring rather than for it involves, the associated aspirations can be a siren song. We can be drawn to look for things in the future. But what we see there simply reflects our implicit assumptions about the nature of the future and is thus subject to the inherent limitations of our knowledge and reasoning. This chapter tackles these assumptions head on by exploring the questions of the nature of the future and our approach to it.

From necessity to contingency

One predominant conception of the future portrays it as something outside of us, unfolding with law-like necessity. Even though this necessary process may itself be uncertain, the point is that we consider ourselves passive recipients of what the process brings. Thus, the reasonable response is to position ourselves against the future for the sake of attaining a beneficial state (Wiltbank et al., 2006). This can be done by focusing either on predicting what the future will be, or on adapting to whatever future arises. Efforts can be directed at developing better prediction models or systems, or at implementing better intelligence and fast response systems.

The relevant point here is that when faced with demands for such activities – such as when someone asks to see market predictions or

financial projections backed by reasonable evidence – we need to acknowledge that their logic is based on an assumption of an external, real future.
This assumption is appropriate for recurrent, already established activities.
Indeed, thinking of realized business opportunities as operating social structures that weave together production and consumption, one can easily see
the overall economy as a super-structure, an inter-linked collection of such
individual structures.

Each structure, once established, becomes a battleground of opposing
forces. One seeks to maintain and even grow the structure – this is the management of the company or venture. Another seeks to disassemble or under-
mine it – the market forces working to steal customers or employees; or the
technology forces that make the production methods obsolete or ineffective.
The former requires energy and effort; the latter occurs naturally, consistent with the tenets of increased entropy (disorder) as a natural tendency of
systems. In this sense, each structure is dissipative in nature (Prigogine,
1997), that is, it requires a flow of external energy to be maintained, such as
retention and reinvestment of earnings, new investment, the renewed efforts
of employees and managers. In the absence of this energy, the structure
will gradually disappear. But it will retain itself for at least a while, just as
an abandoned building will stand for some time before crumbling down
completely.

Therefore, and particularly in view of the ongoing efforts to maintain it,
each structure offers a good position – a fort of sorts – against the future. It
enables relatively reliable prediction based on extrapolation from past activity and on its intended perpetuation and expansion. It also enables effective,
incremental, piecemeal adaptation as new elements are added in response
to changes in the environment. Think of the analogy of a building that gets
gradually adapted to changing climate, demographics, or use. There is continuity and stability in the short term and more substantive changes in the
longer term.

In other words, positioning works for existing structures. But a new venture is oriented towards the creation of a new structure. Even when this
involves use of elements of existing structures – such as factory or retail
infrastructure or current customer relationships – through their acquisition,
retention, or replication, there are always new elements to be added to complete and activate the structure. This does not yet offer a solid foundation for
positioning. Any prediction or adaptation is in effect an out-of-range extrapolation. But more importantly, the very attempt to erect a new structure
represents a disturbance to the existing economic super-structure because
the elements it aims to pull together are engaged in other, already active
structures. Prospective customers or employees have current commitments
for their time and money. These commitments have to be disrupted and
subsumed in the new structure. As such, the new structure becomes part

of the incoming future and invites adaptive responses as well as proactive moves by others.

In this setting, it is prudent to consider an alternative conception of the future, in which it is emergent and contingent, where our actions matter through the reactions and consequences they trigger. Our actions are motivated by a certain purpose, but it is difficult to think ahead more than a few steps because of the exponential expansion of the number of contingent actions that require consideration. Consider the simple example of being in the middle of an infinite chess board. There are 8 possible squares where we can land after one move, 25 possible squares after two moves, and 49 possible squares after three moves. If we then add another person on the board and consider our relative positions after each step, there are 64 possibilities after one move, 625 possibilities after two moves, and 2401 possibilities after three moves. After adding a third person, the possibilities become 512; 15,625; and 117,649 respectively. In real settings, there are more than three players to consider. We simply cannot think of all the possibilities more than a few moves ahead.

At any point in time, the future is an uncountable range of possibilities, only one of which could materialize. The question of which one will transpire is open ended, subject to competing visions and actions. If we stand still, something will still happen. But it is also reasonable to presume that if we do something, something different will happen. In this sense, we have a stake in the future, even if what actually happens is not within our control.

A contingent future means that it can turn out differently in (slightly) different circumstances. Thinking about the future, we are interested in three things that comprise it: (1) the events that will happen, (2) their consequences in terms of further events their trigger as well as their meanings, and (3) the preferences that people will exhibit, which will drive their economic decisions. Even if certain events can be foreseen, their consequences are difficult to anticipate due to the social complexity of our world. This is the difference between prediction and prophecy, what happens versus what it means (Watts, 2011). Similarly, it is difficult to ascertain future preferences: choices can drive preferences as much as preferences can drive choice (March, 1978). In the words of Henry Ford, "If I had asked people what they wanted, they would have said faster horses".

The distinction between perceiving the future as driven by necessity vs. contingency is important because of how we deal with the uncertainty that surrounds it. Against a future shaped by necessity, we place the uncertainty inside ourselves, that is, we are uncertain about the future. Removing the uncertainty from ourselves becomes a quest for more information and analysis, with the hope that the future will reveal itself or become more clear. In contrast, against a future shaped by contingency, we place the uncertainty outside ourselves, meaning the future itself is uncertain. Removing the uncertainty becomes a matter of eliminating competing possibilities. We have a stake in this matter through what we want and are willing to see through. But this matter is ultimately sorted at a macroscopic level – what happens is derived from what all actors do. We are but one of many inter-connected actors.

Action principles for contingency

The power of contingency lies in the fact that things can take a turn for the better or for the worse at each step of the way. Each new step thus brings both hope and danger, just like reaching a milestone or looking around a corner. When we cannot look more than a few steps ahead, the journey becomes a matter of reaching milestone after milestone, each opening a new vista with new directions and further milestones. In view of this, there are two main principles that can guide us: (1) the ability to reach the next milestone and (2) the ability to change direction. In turn, each of these is subject to both internal and external pressures and considerations. This gives rise to four sets of principles as shown in Table 5.1.

Reaching the next milestone

The ability to reach the next milestone is typically associated with persistence, the stamina to keep going. Indeed, most entrepreneurial success stories talk about persistence and most aspiring entrepreneurs exhibit a sense of hope that success is just around the corner. But there is more to persistence than meets the eye. As with any action, it brings an interplay of motivation and ability, a desire to keep going as well an ability to do so. These can be subject to both internal and external pressures.

The internal pressures or considerations have to do with wanting to get to the next milestone. This desire can reflect the pull of the ultimate goal: of what we hope to achieve in the end. It can also reflect the intrinsic enjoyment

Table 5.1 Action principles for contingent future

	Considerations/pressures	
	Internal	*External*
Getting to the next milestone	Intrinsic logic Living with uncertainty	Affordability
Changing direction	Structural openness Planning vs. plan	Decision control Dynamic commitments

or 'psychic income' received from the activity itself, or the opportunity costs of our time and effort (Gimeno et al., 1997). We thus revisit the questions posed earlier in the book, of whether our engagement in entrepreneurship is driven by the outputs it can produce or its very process. In the former case, satisfaction is uncertain, while in the latter it is guaranteed. After several milestones, the extrinsic pull may diminish, weighed down by an ever-opening stretch of new milestones or the rising opportunity costs of alternative pursuits. At the same time, the intrinsic push is likely to remain strong as long as one is able to live with the uncertainty of the process. From this point of view, a first action principle can be formulated as intrinsic logic and living with uncertainty. This action principle is developed further in Chapter 7.

The external pressures or considerations have to do with whether we have the energy or resources to get to the next milestone. As discussed earlier, entrepreneurship requires sacrifices. They can easily accumulate in the absence of tangible results. With the expectation that there may be many milestones to come, it is important to maintain the ability to get to yet another one. Giving up can be a source of deep regret, arising from the sense that one more step or push might have been all it would have taken to reach some successful result. To use the analogy of long-distance running, one of the essential skills there is pace, as a fine balance between effort and physiological capacity. The relevant resources in the entrepreneurship space are time and money: getting to the next milestone requires a commitment of time; and it often requires the expense of money, that is to buy equipment, hire people, rent premises, etc. Neither of these are infinite and, once exhausted, we are unable to continue.

Our time is a critical resource in the sense that we can devote it to productive activities that enable us to financially support ourselves and our family. In the absence of alternative means of support, such as savings or family support, there is a limited amount of time that we can endure without earning an income. Similarly, within an employment setting, there is limited amount of time we can devote to other, non-job-related activities, before our job performance is considered unsatisfactory. The same logic applies to financial resources. There is a limit to how far we can deplete our stock or even stretch it into the negative, such as when we borrow money. The limit is driven by our own personal financial needs, lifestyle aspirations, and ability to repay the borrowings.

What matters then, for both time and money, is that the limits in question represent thresholds of affordability. Crossing the threshold puts us in danger of suffering the negative consequences of financial hardship, job loss, or bankruptcy. The principle of affordable loss pertains to the need to determine and face the worst-case scenario in any endeavour and ensure that it is something affordable (Sarasvathy, 2001). Thus, the second action principle can be formulated as affordability. It will be developed further in Chapter 8.

Changing direction

The ability to change direction requires flexibility to reconsider our approach and our options as well as ability to reflect on our journey so far and consider going back to take a different turn. As with the ability to continue, it is subject to both internal and external pressures that need to be kept in check. Not showing flexibility can arise from inability either to see new possibilities or to pursue these possibilities. The former reflects internal constrains while the latter external.

The internal constraints pertain to our perceived roadmap or plan for the journey. To the extent that it is rigid, demanding disciplined execution, it would see any change of direction as unnecessary deviation. In this regard, the need for flexibility reflects the importance of being able to escape any structure imposed on the entrepreneurial process, of seeing any such structure as ultimately tentative. Creating a structure is an essential component of execution and efficiency: it enables coordination, communication, and decision making. But its effectiveness ultimately hinges upon having a well-defined goal or destination for the venture: the very thing that the entrepreneurial journey is after.

Much has been written about business plans and their use in the entrepreneurial process. The business plan, as a document, once written, can easily become an anchor point, a source of focus and discipline, a sort of attentional structure that defines goals and responsibilities. There is no denying its value once it is clear what the venture aims to achieve, once its opportunity is clear enough. But in the early stages of the entrepreneurial process, it is the process of planning rather than the plan itself that plays a positive role (Dimov, 2010). In the context of the exploration and experimentation inherent to these early stages, the rigid structure of a plan can create blindspots in that new information can be easily ignored as irrelevant. The plan itself acts as a filter and a source of meaning.

In contrast, an ongoing process of planning can be seen as a continuous reassessment of the new possibilities that previous actions open up. It aims to structure what is known so far, as a way of identifying promising next steps, new assumptions, and ways of verifying them. But that structure is never final, only tentative, ready to be recast at the next step. The structure thus helps make sense of the journey so far and anticipate the journey ahead.

It creates a continuity among the steps taken, enabling us to retrace these steps and explore previous structures in the light of new information. Without any structure, there is chaos. Thus, the third principle can be formulated as structural openness and planning vs. plan. It will be developed further in Chapter 7.

The external constraints pertain to whether we are in a position to decide or institute a move in a new direction; that is, it is a question of decision rights. From a property rights point of view, there are two types of rights associated with the venture: income rights relate to claims on the ultimate residual profits from the venture; decision rights relate to how the venture is developed and managed (Hart and Moore, 1990). While these rights are initially concentrated in the venture founders, they can be gradually given away as other stakeholders are involved, such as investors and employees. To the extent that there are other decision makers involved, the question of which direction to follow is subject to discussion or debate, the outcome of which is not entirely down to our own preferences.

While the sacrifices associated with the venture are initially our own time and resources, the need to obtain additional resources – whether financial, manpower, or expertise – demands sacrifices from others. To elicit these sacrifices, we have to create attachments or commitments in the form of promises, plans, or investments that involve other people. This creates a new reality in the present that is vested in things turning out in a certain way and that becomes separate from us as it is communicated to and seen by others. As others become vested in that reality, they can demand control over whether and how it comes about.

The negotiation with investors and other stakeholders over the conditions in which they would commit their resources can be complex and involve an interplay between income and decision rights. Similar to the business plan, these conditions can be seen as a sort of structure of rights and obligations that is aimed at ensuring that the desired end comes about. But when the end is not yet well defined, and is expected to evolve in the early stages of the journey, the structure should not be rigid but flexible, giving us the ability to consider a new direction or a new approach. Thus, the fourth principle can be formulated as decision control and dynamic commitments. It will be developed further in Chapter 8.

In summary, viewing the future as contingent calls for action principles that keep future options open. Four sets of principles are summarized in Figure 5.1. They pertain to the ability to reach the next milestone and the ability to change direction, to be maintained under continuous internal and external pressures. Chapter 6 discusses the nature of the milestones in the entrepreneurial journey. Chapters 7 and 8 focus on managing the internal and external pressures.

References

Dimov, D. (2010). 'Nascent entrepreneurs and venture emergence: Opportunity confidence, human capital, and early planning'. *Journal of Management Studies*, **47**(6), 1123–1153.

Gimeno, J., Folta, T.B., Cooper, A.C. and Woo, C.Y. (1997). 'Survival of the fittest? Entrepreneurial human capital and the persistence of underperforming firms'. *Administrative Science Quarterly*, **42**(4), 750–783.

Hart, O. and Moore, J. (1990). 'Property rights and the nature of the firm'. *Journal of Political Economy*, **98**(6), 1119–1158.

March, J.G. (1978). 'Bounded rationality, ambiguity, and the engineering of choice'. *The Bell Journal of Economics*, **9**(2), 587–608.

Prigogine, I. (1997). *The end of certainty: Time, chaos, and the new laws of nature.* New York: Free Press.

Sarasvathy, S.D. (2001). 'Causation and effectuation: Toward a theoretical shift from economic inevitability to entrepreneurial contingency'. *Academy of Management Review*, **26**(2), 243–263.

Watts, D.J. (2011). *Everything is obvious: Once you know the answer.* New York: Crown Business.

Wiltbank, R., Dew, N., Read, S. and Sarasvathy, S.D. (2006). 'What to do next? The case for non-predictive strategy'. *Strategic Management Journal*, **27**(10), 981–998.

6 Milestones and problems

Dealing with a contingent future shifts the emphasis to more immediate milestones. While our ultimate purpose is reflected in a vision of a desired future, rather than passively prophesy about it, we have to try to bring it about bit by bit, conscious that around us there are competing visions for alternative futures. In identifying more immediate milestones, we have to maintain a sense of relationship between each milestone and the ultimate purpose and among the different milestones, into one coherent whole. This chapter offers a framework for understanding the milestones and their inter-relatedness.

Business model as a keystone to the journey

Chapter 1 discussed the nature of the realized opportunity as a social structure (Figure 1.1) encompassing a product or service, users or customers, and a production infrastructure and stakeholders. At first, these elements are imagined, as contained and articulated in the original business idea. The entrepreneurial journey seeks their validation, which most of the time results in their modification around what turns out to be possible or feasible. There comes a point in the journey when there is sufficient confidence in the feasibility and realization of the structure. Beyond that point, the journey becomes a question of execution, of building the structure. This is not a trivial problem, but one that requires focus and discipline, in contrast to the open-ended validation process.

The so-determined structure represents the business model for the venture. Just as an architectural model represents a keystone to a building design effort, ensuring that a prospective building would serve its intended purpose, so a model of the business represents a keystone in the entrepreneurial journey. Once validating the elements of the future structure, it provides a focus for the remainder of the journey. In this regard, the entrepreneurial journey has two qualitatively different phases – search and execution (Blank and

Dorf, 2012) – with the construction/validation of a viable business model representing the transition point between the two. Getting to that point is a process of iteration and experimentation, of finding out what works, transitioning between different business models until settling down on one that works (Mullins and Komisar, 2009).

It is useful here to draw the distinction between business model and business plan, given the wide and often confusing use of both terms. The architecture analogy helps draw that distinction most clearly. The business model is the equivalent of the architectural model: a physical (or virtual) representation of a structure aimed to visualize or communicate its design and to determine the fulfilment of its purpose and its technical or cost viability. In turn, the business plan is the equivalent of the construction or project plan: it is put in place once the building design is approved for execution. The business model thus represents a viable blueprint, while the business plan is concerned with its execution.

The keystone nature of the business model is well captured by the words of the architect Frank Lloyd Wright: "It is easier to use an eraser on the drafting table than a wrecking ball on the building site". Creating a blueprint is a difficult process that seeks to integrate what is desired with what is technically possible and financially viable. Once the blueprint is ready, the process of its execution or realization is equally difficult as it requires planning, coordination, quality control, monitoring of progress and costs, and responding to unanticipated setbacks. These are two sets of qualitatively different activities.

The business model in effect determines whether it is worth for others to take the venture seriously. It represents an inter-subjective agreement about the merits of the venture – no longer simply the product of our imagination, but validated by the beliefs and commitments of others. In the absence of it, significant doubts remain and are difficult to dissipate. It is notable that in the parlance of venture capital, the first venture funding round (Series A) hinges upon the start-up's having a clear business model. The stages prior to that – referred to as pre-seed or seed – signal that a start-up is still in the process of defining or validating its business model.

Business model as tripartite, wicked problem

As a representation of the prospective venture, what does a business model consist of? Although the seeming foundation of a business is the core value it delivers through its product or service to its set of customers, this needs to be considered in conjunction with the desired quality of the product and the overall financial viability of the endeavour. Thus, the business model has three main elements: a customer interface, a production infrastructure, and a financial model. These are reflected in the popular business model canvas, which further breaks these elements into nine building blocks for the business (Osterwalder and Pigneur, 2009).

These three elements define three major problems that each business model has to solve: (1) market desirability, that is there needs to be actual demand for the product or service in the market; (2) technical or operational feasibility, that is the product or service needs to be made of a requisite quality and price; and (3) financial viability, that is there needs to be a positive balance between revenues and costs and its accumulation should recover the investments made to set up the venture (Dimov, 2016). The solution to these problems, meaning identifying a point that satisfies all three, is a tripartite design problem, as illustrated in Figure 6.1.

The tripartite nature of the problem means that, while it may be easy to solve any of the individual parts of the problem, it is vastly more difficult to solve all three because of the way these individual problems are interconnected. Making improvement on one can worsen the status of another. Thus, we can determine what prospective customers want, only to discover that this is impossible or too expensive to deliver. We can then reduce costs by removing features, only to discover that customers are not willing to pay for this as much as we hoped.

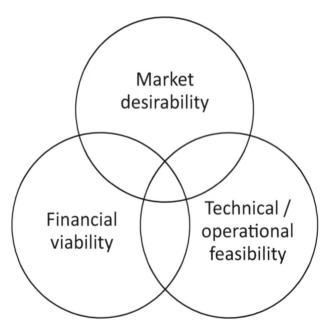

Figure 6.1 Entrepreneurial design problem.

Source: Adapted from Dimov (2016).

This is a typical example of an ill-structured or wicked problem, also known as design problem. Unlike structured problems that are clearly defined and have a single, optimal solution for which some sort of generic problem-solving algorithm can be derived, wicked problems are ill-defined and thus have no clear or optimal solution. They arise in socially complex settings, with multiple points of view and interdependent behaviours. This means that different observers can see different problems to be solved in a given situation, and the piecemeal attempt to solve any of these problems can exacerbate or create other problems.

More broadly, wicked problems have several key features, as discussed by Rittel and Webber (1973) in their classic paper. First, they have no definitive formulation and are thus susceptible to multiple framings based on the viewpoint and priorities of the various observers. Thus, we can easily imagine that some people will choose to tackle marketing problems, others operational or technological, and yet others financial or human resource problems.

Second, and perhaps most crucial, the formulation of the problem often does not arise until a solution is proposed. When given a prototype solution, users can identify problems associated with its use and suggest various ways in which it could be improved. None of these could have been articulated without first trying out the prototype. This reflects the essential role that a prototype plays in a design process – to suggest new possibilities based on the reactions it elicits.

The broader point here is that, while the terms 'product' and 'customer' are well established and seemingly clear, it is not clear which one comes first given their relational nature. We can think of people as customers only in respect to a particular product (otherwise, they would be just people). And we can think of something as a product only in respect to some potential users (otherwise it would be just a gadget). We can break away from this vicious circle by taking an arbitrary starting point: either a group of people, looking to identify something of potential interest to them; or something with potential functional uses or benefits, looking to identify potential users for it. By looking to bring the two parts together, we set off on an expanding spiral of possibilities.

Third, wicked problems have no stopping rule: there is no clear sense of when the problem is solved. The set of potential solutions is not enumerable, which makes it impossible to derive an optimum solution. As a consequence, solutions are judged not as right or wrong, but as good or bad, depending on the results achieved. This mirrors the evaluation judgment discussed earlier, focusing on whether a solution works and the possibilities it opens.

Finally, every problem is novel and unique, reflecting the distinct situation and time period in which it occurs. In this sense, attempted solutions work as one-shot operations in the sense that, once enacted, they change the situation in an irreversible way. That is, it is impossible to reset the process and try a different direction from the same set of initial conditions. If an attempted solution gives rise to new problems, these then become part of the problem situation going forward.

The reality of wicked problems bites from the outset of the entrepreneurial journey in the sense of not knowing what knowledge and information are relevant for the journey ahead (Sarasvathy et al., 2008). Indeed, we could see every piece of information as potentially relevant as we can project it onto the problem. Thus, our essential role in the entrepreneurial process is to make sense of its undefined situations, to structure or frame them into something that we can dealt with, to turn them from indeterminate to determinate. This activity rests on a set of beliefs, tacit assumptions, or working principles that are tentative.

In the light of the broad action principles defined in the previous chapter, there are two implications for how the process can be managed going forward. Maintaining the tentative nature of our situational sense making poses internal (to ourselves) challenges associated with accepting the inherent uncertainty of the process and with changing our frames of reference. It also poses external challenges associated with keeping at bay the certainty and frames that are imposed by others in the context of our resource exchange relationship with them. These internal and external challenges are addressed in the next two chapters.

References

Blank, S. and Dorf, B. (2012). *The startup owner's manual*. Pescadero, CA: K&S Ranch Press.

Dimov, D. (2016). 'Toward a design science of entrepreneurship'. In A.C. Corbett and J.A. Katz (Eds.), *Advances in entrepreneurship, firm emergence and growth*. Bingley, UK: Emerald Insight, Vol. 18, 1–31.

Mullins, J. and Komisar, R. (2009). *Getting to plan B: Breaking through to a better business model*. Boston, MA: Harvard Business Press.

Osterwalder, A. and Pigneur, Y. (2009). *Business model generation*. Hoboken, NJ: Wiley.

Rittel, H.W.J. and Webber, M.M. (1973). 'Dilemmas in a general theory of planning'. *Policy Sciences*, **4**(2), 155–169.

Sarasvathy, S.D., Dew, N., Read, S. and Wiltbank, R. (2008). 'Designing organizations that design environments: Lessons from entrepreneurial expertise'. *Organization Studies*, **29**(3), 331–350.

7 Managing internal pressures

The previous two chapters portray a process in which it is possible to lose our grounding or sense of progress. Viewing the future as contingent calls for an open-ended, step-by-step approach. Our ultimate purpose is translated into more immediate milestones that we tackle as our next step, reassessing our direction and approach after each attempt. But these milestones are part of an elusive target – a proven business model – the elements of which form a wicked configuration. What matters at any single point in time is whether we can keep going and whether we can manoeuvre out of dead ends. Needless to say, frustration can build up quickly, with no firm pointers onto which to grab. This chapter focuses on managing this internal pressure.

To keep the process going is a matter of motivation. When this motivation is extrinsic, anchored in a specific ultimate outcome we aim to achieve, it may diminish as the journey protracts and its destination proves ever elusive. In contrast, finding an internal compass that puts emphasis on the experience itself (rather than outcomes) can keep the motivation steady. But it cannot eliminate the uncertainty in which the journey is enshrined in terms of its ultimate realization. This raises the issue of living with such uncertainty.

Changing direction is a matter of how we determine what is appropriate to do in the light of the latest milestone or outcomes. To the extent that we have a rigid roadmap, a new approach or direction can be ruled out as inappropriate. The roadmap arises from an implicit framing of the situation in terms of what problem we aim to solve and how to solve it. The frame represents an attentional structure that sorts information into relevant and irrelevant. As we strive to maintaining structural openness, the issue arises of recognizing our own self-imposed constraints.

Living with uncertainty

The entrepreneurial journey is inherently uncertain, giving rise to the three tensions discussed in the first part of the book. This uncertainty cannot be eliminated, in the sense of knowing where we will end up. We have to live with it, pursuing milestone after milestone. At any point, we are at the forefront of the line of time, having charted the history of our efforts so far but facing a web of dotted lines ahead. In this sense, the imaginary milestone ahead lies across time not yet passed. The uncertainty surrounding it arises only when we think about it, trying to look for certainty that we will reach it.

There is no uncertainty in immediate experience, in what Henry Bergson calls 'pure duration', as an inter-penetrating multiplicity of present and past moments (1913). In this regard, by focusing on the intrinsic enjoyment or passion associated with the entrepreneurial experience itself, we stay within pure duration. This means that we can work towards the next milestone without seeking affirmation that this will result in particular outcomes. We simply follow the flow of passion, finding justification for what we do in the activity itself rather than in what it may bring.

Uncertainty arises only when we start thinking about what may happen outside of our present moment, ahead of it. This thinking process takes us out of the immediacy of our experience, extending our timeline forward and looking to define our future experience before we actually experience it. But what prompts such thinking? Why can't we just relax and live in the present moment, taking new experiences as they come? Where does the worry about whether we can reach the next milestone come from?

The thinking and worry is related to the possibility that our own vision of what lies ahead may turn out to be wrong. When we become vested in the vision, whether through commitment to ourselves or commitment to others, we seek to preserve it and thereby crave certainty, the assurance that it will transpire. The impossibility of such assurance becomes a source of uncertainty. Living with this uncertainty means that we do things without a reliable marker that they are the right things to do. It implies accepting the possibility of being wrong.

Uncertainty can generate fear of taking responsibility for an action, because this makes us vulnerable. This feeling contrasts sharply with the assuredness that emanates from success stories, recounting difficult decisions in the light of their eventual pay-off. The contrast between the retrospective certainty and prospective uncertainty in turn may create a feeling of imperfection, of being not being up to the task. This channels itself in seeking advice, of reaching out to experts as a way of shifting the responsibility of what to do to someone else. Needless to say, this activity can generate a lot of noise in that we are bound to hear different opinions and different recommendations.

The work of Brené Brown, who has explored the subject of vulnerability in great depth, suggests that living with uncertainty and its inherent vulnerability call for cultivating shame resilience (2013). One aspect of this is the need to resist external noise by developing internal shelter based on intuition and faith. Intuition refers to "our ability to hold space for uncertainty and our willingness to trust the many ways we've developed knowledge and insight, including instinct, experience, faith, and reason" (Brown, 2010: 89). Faith refers to "a place of mystery, where we find the courage to believe in what we cannot see and the strength to let go of our fear of uncertainty" (90).

Indeed, many entrepreneurs speak of intuition and faith when they describe their journeys and the basis on which they move ahead. Curiously, reflecting on his decision not to take on the iPhone chip, Intel's CEO Paul Otellini said "while we like to speak with data around here, so many times in my career I've ended up making decisions with my gut, and I should have followed my gut. . . . My gut told me to say yes" (Madrigal, 2013: paragraph 10).

Intuition and faith suggest an inward orientation. But taken to the extreme, this orientation can lead to isolation that eventually starts letting in doubt and fear. These create the sense that it is only we that are lost; that it is much easier for others; that everyone else seems to be enlightened and confident in terms of where they are going. Because shame thrives on secrecy and isolation, this is where network relationships can help put things out in the open and thereby dispel the shame clouds that gather inside us.

Some of these relationships involve reaching out to trusted confidants, who can offer support and empathy for our experience. Sharing our deepest fear and doubts offers an important release to the internal pressures building up. In our dealings with the stakeholders we aim to attract – customers, investors, employees, suppliers, partners – we have to project constant optimism and confidence. Otherwise, those relationships will not come through. This is such a fine balance: the very commitments we can gain through our confidence can create momentum for the venture that in turn can build our confidence up further and end up justifying it in the first place. But without those relationships or commitments, the opposite, negative feedback loop can take place: momentum is stalled, confidence is undermined, thereby suggesting we had been wrong to feel confident in the first place. The phrase 'fake it till you make it' is probably too harsh here, but it points to the tension we have to maintain inside, being both confident and doubtful. Seeking support and empathy represents a vital safety valve.

The other use of network relationships relates to connecting with experienced mentors, that is people who have been through this journey before. Their primary role is to recognize that our experience is not unique, that others have gone through the same thing, that it is normal to see at times no light at the end of the tunnel. This helps normalize our experience, making us feel part of the larger community of entrepreneurs. It can also help boost the very confidence we need to secure stakeholder commitments and create momentum for our efforts. Indeed, mentoring is a primary support function in the early stages of the entrepreneurial journey, prevalent in incubators or accelerators, and a key role played by seed-stage investors.

Recognizing self-imposed constraints

In thinking about what to do next, we have a sense of purpose, of what the desired future realization looks like, of what social structure we are aiming to build. The gap between this desired future and our current situation represents a problem to be solved, and it is against this overarching problem that we define the specific problem or milestone to tackle next. The ability to change approach or direction calls for openness in respect to the next path to take. Lack of openness reveals itself in two ways. First, there may be options or possibilities of which we are not even aware because our attention is directed elsewhere. Second, there may be options or possibilities that occur or are suggested to us, but we reject them out of hand for being unreasonable, irrelevant, or unworkable.

It is crucial to recognize that, in looking at our problem situation, we implicitly impose a structure on it. As discussed in Chapter 6, our entrepreneurial action is enabled by making the indeterminate situations we face – in which all information may seem relevant – into determinate ones, so that we can deal with them. Such structuring creates a filter of relevance as well as imposes boundaries for the focus of our attention. It is within such a structure that we consider some paths reasonable, while rejecting others out of hand. But such structuring is self-imposed and ultimately tentative. Thus, while it enables us to deal with the situation immediately, it also represents a self-imposed constraint on how we deal with it.

The entrepreneurial journey constitutes a design challenge: we aim to assemble/construct a business model that works, representing a solution to the tripartite problem of market desirability, technical or operational feasibility, and financial viability. Because this problem is wicked, it has neither a definite formulation nor a pre-determined solution. The formulation and solution co-evolve: a given formulation can suggest a solution, which in turn raises new problems that can lead to different formulations and different solutions; and so on.

The problem formulation or frame is therefore a foundation, from which we seek to derive our solutions. It represents an interlocking of our desired outcome with a set of working principles through which it is to be achieved, that defines the scope and criteria for solution search (Dorst, 2011). Because neither the working principles nor the solution means are given at the start – we face a desired outcome but effectively a blank sheet on how to approach it – we have to identify both, in an open-ended enquiry that Dorst terms 'design abduction' (2011). Solving this challenge requires adopting a set of working principles through which the outcome may be produced and then searching for the appropriate means within that frame. This is illustrated in Figure 7.1.

The key insight here is that any frame is tentative in nature. It is imposed by the observer/entrepreneur rather than being an inherent part of the situation itself. Thus, the frame is often implied in the vision of the entrepreneur but, even then, it is but a set of working principles. When a frame is taken for granted, it is never questioned and, accordingly, the search for solutions operates entirely within it. In contrast, when the tacit assumptions that

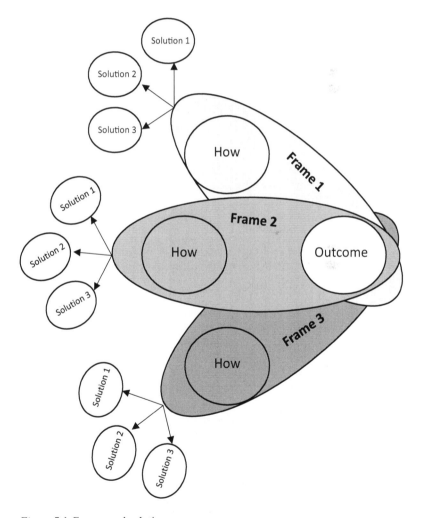

Figure 7.1 Frames and solutions.

comprise it are identified, questioned and reformulated, and the scope for solutions expands significantly in previously unforeseen directions. These two approaches are known respectively as single- and double-loop learning (Argyris and Schon, 1974).

In the problem-solving process, we seek to move forward and to evaluate each action undertaken. There is thus a repertoire of three types of move. The first is developmental, whereby an action is intended to bring closer a solution and the outcome is evaluated. The second is exploratory: an action is intended to generate new possibilities for further action. The third is reframing: a new frame is imposed on the situation. Moves 1 and 2 happen within an existing frame, while move 3 brings about a new frame.

Because these moves can be combined in a single action, the information that an action brings can be evaluated at three different levels: (1) the situation itself, (2) the suitability of the action, (3) the suitability of the frame (Argyris et al., 1985). Therefore, the evaluation of each action should be accompanied by a deeper reflection that can access all these different levels of inference. For example, if an action unsuccessful, there are several possibilities for what to make of this and what to do next. First, we can repeat the action, with the understanding that the first outcome was a fluke, down to some unfortunate circumstances. Second, we can direct the action at a different recipient or repeat it in a different situation. Third, we can choose a different action from within the same set of working principles, directed towards the same recipient. Or, we can modify our understanding of the problem, adding constraints or other contextual factors; or completely re-formulate the problem.

Over time, reflection creates a thread to our path of exploration and enables us to build knowledge of different actions, outcomes, and contexts. This becomes a valuable repertoire that can help us deal with – that is frame and re-frame – new situations (Schon, 1983). The need for reflection speaks to the importance of deferring judgment, of not jumping to immediate conclusions, of building a nuanced understanding of contexts, actions, and framings. Part of that nuanced understanding is the re-definition of our purpose in terms of a broader, central theme that allows new paths – ones that previously may have seen unrelated – to be connected to it. For example, we can think of an Italian restaurant, just restaurant, a dining place, or a place for entertainment. It is the return to this central theme of the journey that enables us to come out of seemingly dead ends and transfer our efforts to a different exploration space.

In summary, being in the entrepreneurial journey creates a number of internal pressures that need to be managed. Living with the uncertainty of the journey calls for coming to terms with our vulnerability by relying on the internal compass of our intuition and faith, and by reaching out to others for support and normalization of our experience. At the same time, we need to maintain a reflective stance that enables us to see the problem we face as a self-imposed frame, to defer judgment, and to build and apply a nuanced understanding that can inform a different view of the situation and open up new paths. While it is easy to get lost in this process, with seemingly nowhere to go after a number of dead ends, the central idea of the journey acts as a base camp to which we can return and from which we can set off in new directions.

References

Argyris, C., Putnam, R. and Smith, D.M. (1985). *Action science: Concepts, methods, and skills for research and intervention.* San Francisco, CA: Jossey-Bass.

Argyris, C. and Schon, D.A. (1974). *Theory in practice: Increasing professional effectiveness.* San Francisco, CA: Jossey-Bass.

Bergson, H. (1913/2001). *Time and free will: An essay on the immediate data of consciousness* [Kindle version]. Mineola, NY: Dover Publications.

Brown, B. (2010). *The gifts of imperfection.* Center City, MN: Hazelden.

Brown, B. (2013). *Daring greatly.* London: Penguin.

Dorst, K. (2011). 'The core of "design thinking" and its application'. *Design Studies*, **32**, 521–532.

Madrigal, A.C. (2013). 'Paul Otellini's Intel: Can the company that built the future survive it?' *The Atlantic*, 16 May 2013. Available at: www.theatlantic.com/technology/archive/2013/05/paul-otellinis-intel-can-the-company-that-built-the-future-survive-it/275825/. Accessed on 3 January 2017.

Schon, D.A. (1983). *The reflective practitioner.* New York: Basic Books.

8   Managing external pressures

The entrepreneurial journey requires resources to keep it going and to build the ultimate social structure of a realized opportunity. This structure, as discussed in Chapter 5, is dissipative in nature: it requires a constant flow of external energy to be sustained. That energy can be simply the human effort required to conduct even the simplest tasks, for example talk to potential customers, negotiate or seek commitments, search for premises, organize people and offices, etc. It can also come from physical resources such as buildings, land, or technology which provide direct benefits to the entrepreneurial effort.

More broadly, the necessary productive resources can be divided into human (manpower or effort); physical (buildings, land, technology); knowledge (know-how); and relational (contacts, referrals). The latter two categories reflect the fact that, often, simple effort is not enough. When that effort is smart or informed – backed by expert knowledge of the context or specific tasks – a lot more can be achieved in the same amount of time. Therefore, it matters who puts in the effort. Similarly, to open doors, obtain commitment, or seal a deal, one often needs a social network referral, a signal of quality, legitimacy, or affiliation. Notably, financial resources are not included here as they, aside from initial working capital, can be considered simply the means to acquire the productive resources listed above. In this sense, financial needs arise as a consequence of the need to acquire specific productive resources.

When all necessary resources are provided by the entrepreneur, the question of fuelling the project does not loom large. This is the case at least at the beginning of the entrepreneurial journey. But as the entrepreneur's means are exhausted, he or she needs to reach out to others, to demand sacrifices or commitments of them. This raises multiple considerations at play as the project becomes subject to the judgment of others. It is thus appropriate to consider the project through the eyes of others and the pressures this creates.

Affordability and play

The principle of affordability outlined in Chapter 5 suggests that the limits of the entrepreneur's time and money represent a threshold of affordability, beyond which the entrepreneur needs to reach out to others. But what does crossing the threshold of affordability really mean? It brings us to the notion of risk taking, often seen as the defining characteristic of entrepreneurs. As risk pertains to the prospect of suffering loss, to take risk means making ourselves vulnerable to that prospect.

But this does not mean that we would actually suffer the loss if we act. Our action is a one-time event that can turn out both well and badly. Once it turns out well, the possibility that it could have turned out badly disappears. But, can this fortunate turn of events vindicate the previously excessive vulnerability to which we had exposed ourselves? Despite the sense of relief that it brings, it certainly cannot serve as a model approach to others, as something to be done again. In gambling, there may be big winners, but we have a good sense not to bet more than we can afford to lose.

Thresholds of affordability vary across individuals: what seems unaffordable (and thus too risky) for one, may be acceptable for another. Thus, the nature of risk taking can be judged only in reference to the person's specific threshold of affordability. There is also the question of whether a person can foresee all the possible negative consequences of his or her action. Some consequences may be accepted knowingly, while others can either loom unbeknownst to us or arise outside of our control. To the extent that knowingly crossing the threshold of affordability can be deemed reckless, the question arises of whether we can draw a distinction between reckless and prudent in the absence of knowing the ultimate consequences to our actions.

The Oxford English dictionary defines reckless as "heedless of danger or the consequences of one's actions", and prudent as "acting with care and thought for the future". Young children sometimes act in what adults may see as reckless manner, not yet having developed the capacity to think ahead and anticipate danger or the consequences of their actions. While some parents can hover over the child's every step, steering away from danger, others can create a safe environment and let the children be themselves. What minor accidents may happen within this safe environment may be considered affordable. Thus, enabling play opens the door to accidents. Avoiding accidents completely means stifling play. Affordability is thus the upper limit of the cost of play.

Children are certainly not reckless. They are curious, playful, exploring, experimenting. It is the natural way to explore and learn about the world. If they see something lying on the road, they would prod it with a stick to see if it would react and how. This exemplifies Kurt Lewin's saying that "one of the best ways to understand the world is to try to change it". As prudency takes over, we lose touch with our child selves as explorers of the world. Our reasoning goes beyond the sense of danger or loss to focus on a cost-benefit analysis, viewing each sacrifice not in the sense of its absolute affordability, but in relation to the benefit it may bring. In the entrepreneurial setting, the cost is clear, but the benefit less so.

Resource balance sheet

As we look for resources beyond our means, it is useful to draw a distinction between the productive resources necessary for developing the venture and the means used to acquire them. This is similar to the way an accounting balance sheet distinguishes assets and liabilities/equity. The former represent the productive assets of a business, and the latter how they are financed (i.e. through debt or equity). Similarly, the means used to acquire resources can be divided into financial and non-financial (in-kind). Using financial means that go beyond the entrepreneur's own capital poses the challenge of identifying and securing sources of funding, whether debt, equity, or grants. Alternatively, the entrepreneur or other partners or stakeholders can provide in-kind contribution of resources, whether effort, physical, knowledge, or referrals.

In-kind contributions of effort can be in the form of volunteered (pro bono) time or in exchange for ownership (sweat equity). Knowledge and relational resources can be accessed when external advisors are used on a pro bono basis for direct input into the decision-making process or for facilitating contacts with customers or suppliers. Similarly, in-kind contributions can also be made in the form of physical resources such as when land, facilities, or technologies are offered for use at no cost. The resource balance sheet is summarized in Table 8.1.

This balance sheet is helpful for two reasons. First, it makes clear that not all dealings and exchanges in the entrepreneurial journey should have a financial basis. Second, because financial capital is concentrated in certain institutions (e.g. banks, pension funds, investment funds), reliance on financial capital implies that these entities have to be brought into the picture,

Table 8.1 Resource balance sheet

Resources	Means of acquisition
Manpower Physical	Financial
Knowledge Relational	In-kind (pro bono partners, sweat equity)

with their own interests, decision processes, and governance and accountability. Thus, for instance, if we need an expert software developer and need the money to pay the person to join our venture, we have to identify and convince the source of money in addition to convincing the developer. In both cases, we need to provide an explanation or justification, but when money is involved, this has to be done with greater rigor, subject to accountability inherent to finance offices or financial institutions.

When we devote our own time and resources, this sacrifice is seamlessly justified by our own sense of hope, purpose, and conviction. But when we demand such sacrifices from others, this sense is difficult to convey to them, for them to experience it in the same way as we do. We need to communicate it and become limited by the means of language. But more crucially, what is up to this point an internal justification must be located externally, in the future realization or impact of the project.

For instance, if we are full-time employees of an organization, we are accountable for our working time in behalf of the organization. Thus, any behaviour that steps outside the boundaries of the job description is, by definition, inappropriate or inefficient. It thus requires justification when we seek authorization for the behaviour from others. From their point of view, they are sacrificing the resource of our time commitment for other purposes and may demand an explicit cost-benefit analysis that calls for the benefit to be articulated and made apparent. Whatever we communicate comes across as a promise, a commitment on our end.

Because money is a versatile resource – it can be put to a wide array of uses – the sacrifice of money is more difficult to justify than the sacrifice of time and effort. Some of the alternative uses of money are readily apparent, whether alternative projects or simply keeping it in a savings account, thereby making its opportunity cost quite explicit. Crucially, aside from the external force of inflation, money is not perishable: if not spent today, it can be preserved for tomorrow. In contrast, effort is time bound – the effort we can extend today is lost once today passes. In view of this, the weight of evidence required for obtaining financial resources is significantly higher. Referring back to Figure 1.2 – which shows that over time solid evidence gradually replaces hope and intuition as the source of conviction in the entrepreneurial journey – the question of timing becomes essential in the resource acquisition process.

Timing

The question of timing relates to balancing the financial needs of the business with its expected value. The expected value of the business is a reflection of the mix between blueprint and realization – the more outstanding tasks there are, the lower the likelihood that they all will be achieved. This reflects the multiplicative nature of the entrepreneurial tasks. Consider the hypothetical example of 20 tasks necessary to complete the venture project, with 10 on each side of the business model milestone, that is, there are 10 tasks to reach from idea to business model and 10 tasks from business model to successful venture. For the first 10 tasks, even if each has a high likelihood of being achieved, say 80 per cent, the overall likelihood of completing all 10 is 10.7 per cent. In other words, roughly one 1 of 10 ideas will reach the business model validation milestone. Once that milestone is reached, if we set the completion likelihood of each of the subsequent ten tasks to 85 per cent, the overall likelihood of completing all 10 is 19.7 per cent, or roughly 1 out of 5. The likelihood of completing all 20 tasks is 2 per cent or 1 out of 50.

This means that, with the completion of the first 10 tasks, the likelihood of success increases approximately 10 times: from 2 per cent to 20 per cent. Against a fixed value of the project (say 100) when all 20 tasks are completed, the increase in the success likelihood means that the expected value of the project increases tenfold with the completion of the first 10 tasks, from 2 to 20. This value increase is related to the elimination of uncertainty – the fact that the 10 tasks in question are no longer outstanding, but completed for sure.

This hypothetical example can be illustrated in two ways, as shown in Figure 8.1. The first is in the form of survival slide, showing the survival rate for each successive set of 10 tasks, starting with an initial set of 100

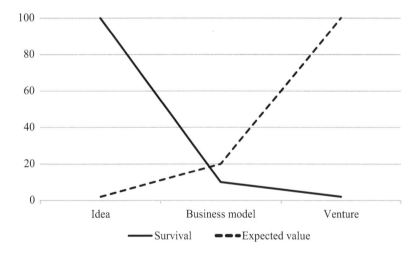

Figure 8.1 Survival slide and expected value climb.

ideas (efforts). The biggest drop is between the onset and the completion of the first 10 tasks, where 90 per cent of the efforts disappear, getting stuck on one of these 10 tasks. Beyond that, the survival drop is still high in relative terms (1 out of 5), but its actual effect is less material because of the lower baseline, that is, going from 100 to 10 feels more drastic than going from 10 to 2.

The second way to illustrate this is in terms of the climb in expected value, working forward towards a realization value of 100. The expected value is the lowest at the outset (2), when all 20 tasks are outstanding. The value increases as tasks get completed and their uncertainty eliminated. Again, although the increase is higher in relative terms after the first 10 tasks (10x vs. 5x), it feels more material in absolute terms in the second stage because of the higher baseline: going from 2 to 20 feels less material than going from 20 to 100. This squares with the discussion in Chapter 6 of the business model as a keystone in the entrepreneurial journey. It also helps understand the practice of venture capital investors of looking for a certain number of completed milestones, that is, venture capital is never the first port of call.

We can easily imagine that where we sit on the precipice of the survival slide has implications for the justification pressure we feel towards others for the sacrifices we demand of them. The pressure is the highest at the very outset, when we have just an idea in hand and face a steep abyss in front. Therefore, we should consider whether and how to bring in resources in a way that is mindful of the survival slide, linking the external viability of the project to the milestones completed.

The first port of call are our own resources, seeking to attain early milestones without the need to look externally. What is important here is that what we sacrifice is deemed affordable, that being caught out in the survival slide will not jeopardize our standing and financial security. Going beyond our own boundaries of affordability, the next port of call would be to secure in-kind contributions. Of course, this requires a creative look at the potential sources, of how the project can be presented in terms of mutual benefit, and of the other parties' own boundaries of affordability. In particular, when this entails bringing in partners who would put in sweat equity, the prospect of going for an extended period of time without financial rewards should be given due consideration. We can also look to secure upfront commitments from potential customers or partners – bringing them on as co-creators – which can not only reduce our financial strain, but also create productive contingencies and momentum (Sarasvathy, 2001).

Finally, the last port of call is the acquisition of resources through financial means, in arms-length transactions. This implies being engaged in a formal fundraising process, with the acknowledgement that this is a significant effort and its opportunity cost is re-focusing the effort on achieving some essential milestones. Entrepreneurs often comment that fundraising requires dedication and often puts business development on hold. The point of principle here is that financial needs are not a given, and it should not be taken for granted that the entrepreneur needs to raise money to proceed. The decision processes of potential investors – driven by justification pressures and associated due diligence – can put an overbearing emphasis on evidence. In the early stages of the process, this can be simply unsurmountable. But rather than thinking about the lack of money as the main challenge at this point, it would be more fruitful to think about how to avoid needing money in tackling some of the immediate milestones ahead.

Property rights

As pointed out in Chapter 5, the entrepreneurial venture comes with a set of property rights attached to it. These can be divided broadly into income and decision rights. Income rights relate to the claims to the eventual income streams from the venture. Equity as a token of ownership represents a residual clam on these streams, after all other claims have been satisfied – its profits. In turn, decision rights relate to determining how the venture is developed and managed. These rights are concentrated initially in the venture founders.

However, as we involve other stakeholders – seeking to acquire resources from them – the question arises of what we need to give up in this exchange. By committing resources to us, these stakeholders make sacrifices. Equally, they can expect us to make sacrifices of our own. What is available for us to sacrifice are our property rights. In this regard, the resource exchange can have implications in terms of the demands imposed on us and thus the flexibility with which we can approach the subsequent steps in the entrepreneurial journey. It also has implications for whether our interests are aligned with those of the other party.

There are different layers to the sacrifices we can make, in terms of both our income and decision rights. For income rights, our sacrifices can be in the form of no, fixed, or residual claims. There are no income claims associated with certain grants or gifts. Fixed claims pertain to set financial amounts that are committed from the venture's income streams. These can arise from employment contracts – that is, when in exchange for committing certain amount of their time to the venture, one is entitled to a salary payment. They can also arise from borrowing agreements, when there is pre-specified repayment amount and schedule of payments. Fixed claims have the advantage of enabling the entrepreneur to enjoy the full upside of the business – the residual profits once all commitments have been satisfied, but create distinct financial obligations that require that income or other funding streams be put in place.

Residual income claims arise when the resource contributors expect to receive a share of our eventual profits. This applies both to situations of sweat equity, when partners or key employees exert their effort in expectation of future rather than immediate financial benefits, and to formal equity investments by business angels or venture capitalists. The sharing of income rights is a primary mechanism of aligning the interests of all parties towards the ultimate success of the venture. Their advantage is that they create no immediate financial obligations, but this comes at the expense of sharing the ultimate upside.

In regard to decision rights, there are similar and equivalent layers that represent no, fixed, and residual claims. The lightest form is when we simply have to exercise goodwill, in the sense of conducting our efforts in good faith and due commitment. This applies to situations in which we receive in-kind contributions of resources that may not require formal reciprocal commitments. Such pro bono contributions are made out of goodwill and desire to promote the cause or purpose we pursue. Because they are extended in the name of our purpose, we need to honour its good-faith pursuit.

There can be fixed claims on our decision rights that apply to specific realms of decisions or behaviours. These take the form of specific obligations – what we have to do, or negative covenants – what we should not do. Examples of these claims are the reporting or insurance requirements as well as prohibited behaviours or transactions associated with loan agreements. They also include the labour-law obligations arising from taking on employees.

Finally, residual decision rights pertain to cases where our prerogative to act as we see fit is curtailed by the need to have major decisions – in predefined areas – subject to the explicit approval of particular stakeholders such as investors, lenders, or partners. These typically pertain to cases of changing the direction or activities of the business, taking on new investors, or selling the business. In such cases, control over the development of the business is effectively reduced. Thus, giving up residual decision rights represents the most significant curtailing of our flexibility. Because such flexibility may be paramount in the early stages of the journey, we should avoid putting ourselves in situations where control of the business is up for grabs, without consideration of the value of the input from the other party or of how aligned our long-term interests are with theirs. In many cases, experienced investors can offer valuable input into the development of the business, particularly at key junctions.

Table 8.2 below summarizes the above arguments in the form of a property rights balance sheet.

Table 8.2 Property rights balance sheet

Resource acquisition means	Property rights (fixed vs. residual)
Financial	Income (cash flow)
In-kind	Decision (control)

In summary, the need for bringing in external resources and the timing of these infusions can create pressures on both income and decision rights. The earlier into the journey these rights are subject to sharing, the weaker our negotiating position – that is, the more difficult it is to back our conviction with evidence – and thus the more we have to give up. As Wasserman argues, the nature of income and decision rights creates an interplay of rich-versus-king attitudes (2012). The former focuses on preserving income rights, while the latter on preserving decision rights, each at the expense of the other. These attitudes should not be self-serving and should instead seek a productive balance among the roles, relationships, and rewards associated with the venture.

References

Sarasvathy, S.D. (2001). 'Causation and effectuation: Toward a theoretical shift from economic inevitability to entrepreneurial contingency'. *Academy of Management Review*, **26**(2), 243–263.

Wasserman, N. (2012). *The founder's dilemmas: Anticipating and avoiding the pitfalls that can sink a startup.* Princeton, NJ: Princeton University Press.

Part III

The journey from the outside

The previous section discussed principles and considerations associated with navigating the entrepreneurial journey in the face of a contingent future. The focus was on the driving seat of the journey – what we see and experience as entrepreneurs, the situations and problems we may face, and the approaches we may take to resolving them and moving ahead. The overarching focus is on maintaining an ability to continue to the next milestone and flexibility to change direction.

As much as the driving seat is important, we need to recognize that the ultimate results to our efforts are not just down to us. We operate in a complex social system, our behaviours are interdependent with those of others and the behaviours and interests of those we aim to attract and retain within the social structure of our venture are similarly affected by the behaviours of others. In short, the situation is ultimately outside of our control, despite our best efforts.

This section aims to recognize and acknowledge this social complexity and situate our actions in a broader context. Our actions become part of a broader entrepreneurial ecosystem, the vitality of which depends on the efforts of all involved, but in which financial rewards are inevitably skewed, as discussed in Chapter 3. We thus need to strike a balance between our own success and the success of the broader ecosystem, to which our efforts – whether successful or unsuccessful – inevitably contribute.

The focus therefore is on the nature of the broader spirit of entrepreneurship. Chapter 9 draws a parallel between entrepreneurship and sport and the interplay between participation and outcomes. Chapter 10 highlights the process of natural attrition inherent in an entrepreneurial ecosystem and draws implications for how to approach entrepreneurial development.

9　Entrepreneurship as sport

The entrepreneurial journey is one of tensions – idea vs. opportunity, genius vs. lunatic, skill vs. luck – as outlined in the first section of this book. They render it impossible to foresee the path that the pursuit of each idea will take. Although it is easy to trace entrepreneurial successes back to the ideas or circumstances that initiated them, the retrospective clarity of these winding paths offers little assurances for what lies ahead for new ideas.

The journey has to be approached in steps, focusing on the nearest milestone ahead. This requires ability to continue and flexibility to change directions in the light of new information or development. These are under the continuous threat of exercising judgments that would deem our efforts unreasonable. The second section of the book outlined some guiding action principles to manage the internal and external pressures that arise throughout the journey.

Ultimately, however, these principles are about the day-to-day facilitation of the journey, about going one step further. They are not about delivering certainty in regard to the final destination or outcome. These remain as opaque as ever, particularly in the early stages of the process. This reinforces one of the central themes of the book, that ideas cannot be discarded or selected at the start. Their potential is not a matter of judgment – with its inherent limitations of knowledge and inaccessibility of yet-to-unfold, socially complex future – but a matter of finding traction, of their development and execution.

Herein lies yet another fundamental tension of the entrepreneurial processes, namely between the individual and collective perspectives of it. In a collective sense, we know that out of many ideas – all pursued in good faith – some will become successfully realized, and perhaps one or two will bring the radical innovations that change the way we live. History shows that this happens with some predictable regularity. But knowing that something big will happen is not enough to suggest which one of a multitude of fledgling ideas will succeed. And this brings in the individual perspective: each of these ideas is pursued by an individual who hopes and believes that they will be the successful ones. While the collective prediction (someone will be successful) is very reliable, the individual hope can be easily deflated by pointing to its seemingly impossible odds. By the same token, we know that there will be a lottery winner, but a particular participant's hope that he or she will be the winner seems too wishful.

Entrepreneurial success as a collective outcome

The individual vs. collective tension further reveals itself in the fact that there is no collective without the individuals: it is the individuals that make the collective. Thus, although we may like the stability of the collective outcome, this outcome only arises if we have sufficient individuals to make the collective. But if each of them had to exercise reason when deciding whether to participate – based on their rational calculation of the odds of winning – they could easily conclude not to bother. And with no one engaging in entrepreneurship, entrepreneurial successes are sure not to come. With no one participating in the lottery, there is no reward pool to distribute.

What is individually rational can be collectively irrational, and vice versa. In a classic example, economists talk of the paradox of thrift: saving money is good for us individually, but if everyone saves too much, then we all may be worse off because of the shrinking of consumption, its negative effect on economic activity, and ultimately, a reduction of our very incomes. Curiously, the same logic applies to entrepreneurial failure, but the other way around: failing is bad for us individually, but if everyone tries (and many fail), we may be better off overall as there will surely be some impactful successes among us.

To succeed, everything needs to go right; to fail only one thing needs to go wrong. This is the essence of the multiplicative nature of the entrepreneurial process. Together with other social processes such as preferential attachment (as discussed in Chapter 3), it gives rise to long-tail outcomes: a few big successes and many failure or mediocre outcomes. But wide participation is not just about increasing the baseline to which to apply these low odds of success. Participation creates competition and collective learning. Competition drives quest for improvement, for making our product or service better. Collective learning is about learning from the mistakes of others, of observing what does not work or inferring how we can make it work the next time. Collectively, we can explore a much wider opportunity area, test a larger number of business propositions, and thus are more likely to bring about big successes. Those who ultimately succeed benefit from these collective efforts.

This logic suggests that entrepreneurial success is ultimately a collective outcome in that it reflects the vibrancy of the system that produces it. This vibrancy comes from wide participation and breaking down barriers to participation and knowledge sharing. These in turn reflect individual attitudes, broader culture, and institutional support, as illustrated by Feld's example of the Boulder community (2012). Similarly, the classic work of Saxenian (1994) on the differential development of Silicon Valley and Route 128 regions of the United States highlights the same points: while Silicon Valley developed a decentralized, cooperative system, Route 128 remained dominated by individual corporations, fuelled by culture and practices of secrecy, loyalty, and internal development.

The nature of entrepreneurial success as a collective outcome recognizes that every participant in the entrepreneurial ecosystem makes a positive contribution, even if their individual efforts are not successful. They might have made mistakes from which others have learned; or pushed others to work harder; or provided valuable experience to help hone others' expertise.

And yet, there is no recognition of this positive contribution. We rightly celebrate success. Entrepreneurial success has a distinct human face – the founders of the next gazelle or unicorn – with all the attention on them. While their ambition and skills are certainty impressive and demand huge respect, they are not necessarily unique and it is not all about them. In our attributions of success, we fail to appreciate the productive role of the entrepreneurial ecosystem and all its unsuccessful or less successful participants.

This is reflected in the terminology and language we use. When talking about entrepreneurship, we often reserve the title 'entrepreneur' only to those who become successful. Being an entrepreneur implies having successfully started a business or other venture with economic or social impact. And the title stays forever: we say X is an entrepreneur, never X was an entrepreneur. When we rely on ultimate outcomes or achievements, our conception of entrepreneurship subsumes all the fortuitous developments in the process. But rather than think of them as a mechanism that sorts participants into successful and non-successful, it is used to create an aura of exceptional abilities around the winners (the halo effect).

Entrepreneurial participation as its own reward

Entrepreneurship is a competitive endeavour and all standing in it is relative. We have a good sense of what success means, but struggle to label the non-successes. The term failure is often used, but it does not do service to the fact that individual efforts are bounded by the broader ecosystem. Thus, while it is technically true that one has failed in the sense of not having achieved his or her own entrepreneurial goals, it is also true that by collective design not everyone can succeed. In other words, the ecosystem is self-organized to produce a few winners, in the same way that a sports tournament has a fixed number of medallists, regardless of the number of participants. No matter how hard they all work, there will be only one winner.

We therefore need to acknowledge entrepreneurial efforts in a positive sense, without attaching negative labels to its outcomes. This interplay works very well in sport. Big competitions – the Olympics, world championships, etc. – work best when a lot of good athletes compete in them. There will certainly be winners, but for each individual competitor, the odds are smaller than certainty. Yet, it is being in the competition that is the essence of being an athlete. The label applies to anyone who competes, regardless of whether they actually win. Most amazingly, no one fails in sport; they simply do not win. Some will succeed, many will wait for the next tournament(s) and in the meantime draw lessons and look to improve. Everybody is equally appreciated.

Sport works on the principle of broad participation. It is an activity that brings individual enjoyment and is something to which we are exposed at an early age. The spirit of good sportsmanship and competition builds character and instils values. The collective benefit of sport is that, through broad participation in it, we can identify and develop talent and celebrate its achievements on the higher stage.

A similar logic of broad participation can apply to entrepreneurship, and exposure to it can also occur early on. The focus need not be on venture creation, but on value creation, on solving social, economic, or environmental problems, whether in the community or on a broader scale. The label 'entrepreneur' would then arise from the purpose one pursues rather than be based on the outcomes one achieves. In this regard, entrepreneurship classes would be like sports classes, involving direct experience and coaching/mentoring, with a focus on improving and competing for the collective benefit, while celebrating individual achievements. The more entrepreneurs and competitions there are, the more winners there will be.

Just like the spirit of sportsmanship, the spirit of entrepreneurship can endure through life. Those carrying the spirit can, aside from venturing on their own, be vital catalysts within communities, established companies, or governments for the creation of culture of innovation, a constant pursuit of improvement.

References

Feld, B. (2012). *Startup communities*. Hoboken, NJ: John Wiley & Sons.
Saxenian, A.L. (1994). *Regional advantage: Culture and competition in Silicon Valley and Route 128*. Cambridge, MA: Harvard University Press.

10 Entrepreneurial impact as emergent development

With the wide participation in entrepreneurship comes yet another tension, namely related to the resource support that can be offered. Resources are ultimately scarce and not unlimited. The money to be offered is limited, and the number of mentors or advisors and the time they can dedicate are also limited. If every idea had to be backed by money or paired up with a mentor, then entrepreneurship would become a very costly endeavour. This forces us to be selective. And yet, we now know that picking winners at the start is very difficult, if not impossible. To resist the temptation of choice, we have to let the winners emerge.

We can think of entrepreneurship as a marathon with many intermediate hurdles. The fact that all hurdles need to be overcome leads to the skewed distribution of entrepreneurial outcomes and the lower odds of completing all hurdles (as discussed in Chapter 8). If the argument in the previous chapter is that everyone should be let into the marathon, then how can we reconcile this with the need to use our scarce resources as a society to achieve maximum entrepreneurial impact?

The entrepreneurial marathon takes place over time, and time – with all the contingencies it brings – brings naturally an attrition and sorting among the participants. While everybody is levelled at the start, not everybody overcomes the first hurdle, even fewer overcome the second, and so on. By the time we reach the substantive hurdle of a viable business model, only a small subset of the participants remain. They have the momentum and represent the biggest promise for achieving entrepreneurial impact. Accordingly, we can offer them the support to get through the next hurdle. Of course, not all will make it through that hurdle. But those who do could in turn be supported through the next stage.

In this way, we harness the natural attrition of entrepreneurial efforts, offering support at each step of the way. As their number dwindles, the support per individual effort increases. It becomes more concentrated and focused on the specific hurdles ahead. This mechanism already exists in sport, as support is funnelled from community participation to elite programmes. At a community level, the support is to encourage wide participation through which talent could be spotted. This is then organized at more intensive teams or competition leagues that enable the talent to be developed further. Eventually, a smaller set of elite athletes emerges that enables concentrated focus on achieving peak, world-beating performance.

We can think of three broader stages of ideation, incubation, and acceleration across which to enable natural attrition of entrepreneurial efforts and provide increasingly concentrated support. Ideation focuses on the generation and initial refinement of entrepreneurial ideas. Incubation focuses on the design of a viable business model, with all the validation of its component and, if necessary, of market potential. The ultimate validation of that model is the successful launch of the venture on some small scale. Acceleration focuses on building up on the small-scale success and scaling up the venture for a wider impact. It is at the acceleration stage that private capital is most available. By that point, most of the initial uncertainties around an idea have been eliminated, and the task ahead is one of disciplined execution.

This mini ecosystem can be activated by setting the hurdles for transition from one stage to the other. These hurdles can be adjusted over time, based on learning from experience. For the sake of an illustrative example, we can have 100 entrepreneurial ideas, of which 20 make it through to incubation and 5 ultimately make it through to acceleration. If we then have a certain pool of resources – say £3 million to support this ecosystem – we need to decide how to allocate them across the three stages.

In the absence of distinguishing the three stages and thereby enabling a process of natural attrition, this support programme could easily turn ineffective. For instance, it could be designed as supporting 100 entrepreneurial ideas with £30k each. Because £30k is not enough to launch a successful venture, the result of this approach would be that the few ventures that do gain significant traction would need additional resources to get to the acceleration stage. But we have no additional resources to offer them, having already allocated our entire budget. In this way, they get stuck as they are not yet investment ready, that is, external investor would not yet be interested.

Furthermore, £30k is too much to spend on ruling out some of the initial ideas; this can be done with a much smaller initial effort or expense. In addition, because of the accountability associated with the £30k support, there might be an inclination to introduce a rigid selection process, with extensive documentation of the idea and even detailed financial projections. This will not only prevent many potential participants from applying, but also inadvertently place incremental, status-quo ideas at an advantage, because their projections are likely to seem more credible. The more radical ideas need resources to simply get to the stage of being credible for this selection process. The result is that entrepreneurship is restricted to a very small exploration space.

By introducing staged support, the ability of the system to explore more widely is greatly increased. Table 10.1 shows two scenarios for allocating

Table 10.1 Supporting entrepreneurial efforts

| | £3m to be allocated to projects | | |
| | | Staged | |
	All in one go	*Equal* *(£1m per stage)*	*Weighted* *(10%–40%–50%)*
Idea (100)	£30k	£10k	£3k
Incubation (20)	£0	£50k	£60k
Acceleration (5)	£0	£200k	£300k
Per accelerated	£30k	£260k	£363k

the £3m support across the three stages, both compared with the equal, undifferentiated allocation discussed above. The first is based on equal allocation and the second on weighted allocation, with higher weighting for the incubation and acceleration stages.

In the first scenario, the £1m to support ideation comes down to £10k per effort; the £1m devoted to incubation then comes down to £50k per incubated venture; and the £1m to support acceleration comes down to £200k per accelerated venture. Thus, the five ultimate successes received £260k in support across the three stages. With the weighted allocation of the second scenario – 10 per cent for ideation, 40 per cent for incubation, and 50 per cent for acceleration – the support for the ultimately successful ventures increases. Each ideation effort receives £3k, each incubated venture receives £60k, and each accelerated venture receives £300k. The total support for each accelerated venture is £363k.

These numbers can be adjusted as necessary to fit particular purposes. But they illustrate how the design of the support system can be used to concentrate resource support on the efforts with the biggest potential, when that potential (1) cannot be ascertained at the start and (2) depends on a wide participation at the start. This is the ultimate strategy for crossing the 'valley of death', by placing charging stations at specific points throughout the valley, each providing a sufficient charge to reach the next station, while also anticipating that fewer and fewer efforts will make it across the way.

There is often talk in policy circles about market failure for entrepreneurial finance. It is based on the observation that there are ideas looking for capital and capital looking for ideas, but the two do not easily meet and merge. What this view fails to consider is that the ideas and capital are separated by a chasm, the 'valley of death', and that this chasm lies not in space but in time. Time acts as a sifter.

Conclusion

Entrepreneurship is ultimately about facing up to the future, about leaving our own creative mark. It takes place in a world that is perpetually evolving, in an economy that exists in perpetual novelty generated through its continuous co-evolution with technology (Arthur, 2009). It is a journey into the unknown – created by its interlinkage with many constantly moving parts – fuelled by purpose and hope. While many would say that being an entrepreneur is all about bravery and action, this book seeks to carve out space for thought and reflection, echoing the words of Henry Bergson, "think like a man of action, act like a man of thought". This is the essence of an entrepreneurial mindset.

It is not easy to think about entrepreneurship. After all, a theory is a sort of intellectual taming, of containing an object or situation in our mind, of extracting it from the flow of experience, of trying to stop time to take a closer look. Think of trying to take a close-up picture of people running towards us: we run ahead, turn back, shoot; then run ahead again, turn back, and shoot. We have to keep running. And our picture turns old the very moment it is taken.

Thinking needs to happen within entrepreneurship. In needs to zoom in and out, keeping track of the world within and at the same time maintaining the perspective of the world outside, a small cog in a wider interconnected system. It also needs to look ahead rather than backwards. But there is nothing ahead – the future has not yet happened – other than our own projection. It needs to be reconciled with the reality of the future as it arises. It is about active perception intertwined with reflection.

Such thinking requires a wide arsenal of perspectives. Accordingly, the book provides a synthesis of insights from a wide range of academic disciplines, each offering a distinct viewpoint for the entrepreneurial journey. The ideas from complexity science, physics, network theory, economics, and social policy help shape our systemic view of the journey. The ideas from design science, action science, business, and management help shape our view of the tasks and problems at hand. The ideas from social and cognitive psychology help develop our awareness of our own thought and emotional processes, as well as those of the stakeholders we seek to engage.

The first part of the book reinforces the need for active perception and reflection – not taking anything for granted – by discussing three constant tensions of the entrepreneurial journey, namely idea vs. opportunity, genius vs. lunatic, and skill vs. luck. It then highlights the limitations of judgment based on the knowledge blindspots that underpin them and outlines two productive roles for judgment that need to work in unison to regulate the tensions.

The second part of the book introduces the idea of a contingent future – one that can turn out differently through different actions and in different circumstances – and outlines two general action principles to help face it: getting to the next milestone and changing direction. It then traces the milestones to the journey to the elements of a business model, intertwined in a tripartite design problem of market desirability, technical or operational feasibility, and financial viability. In the pursuit of this wicked problem, we have to deal with internal pressures related to enduring the uncertainty of the process and recognizing our own self-imposed constraints, as well as with external pressures related to maintaining affordability and decision control.

The third part of the book situates entrepreneurial efforts in a broader entrepreneurial ecosystem in search of appreciation for entrepreneurship beyond the simple and misleading dichotomy of success and failure. Applying the analogy of sport enables us to catalyze the interplay between participation and outcomes, while harnessing the natural attrition associated with the process offers implications for how to support entrepreneurial development.

The book naturally raises more questions than answers. Questions are a powerful tool: they help dislodge and loosen existing preconceptions and prepare the ground for a new, entrepreneurial mindset as well as give rise to new opportunities. The mindset would not arise from simply reading the book but, gradually, through the reflective practice it enables. Although some of the points made in the book may ring too abstract at this point, they will start making concrete sense as you set off on your entrepreneurial journey and begin experiencing its tensions and pressures. Bon voyage!

I hope you have enjoyed reading the book as much as I have enjoyed writing it.

Reference

Arthur, W.B. (2009). *The nature of technology: What it is and how it evolves*. London: Allen Lane.

Bibliography

Andriani, P. and McKelvey, B. (2009). 'From Gaussian to Paretian thinking: Causes and implications of power laws in organizations'. *Organization Science*, **20**(6), 1–19.

Argyris, C., Putnam, R. and Smith, D.M. (1985). *Action science: Concepts, methods, and skills for research and intervention*. San Francisco, CA: Jossey-Bass.

Argyris, C. and Schon, D.A. (1974). *Theory in Practice: Increasing professional effectiveness*. San Francisco, CA: Jossey-Bass.

Arthur, W.B. (2009). *The nature of technology: What it is and how it evolves*. London: Allen Lane.

Bergson, H. (1913/2001). *Time and free will: An essay on the immediate data of consciousness* [Kindle version]. Mineola, NY: Dover Publications.

Blank, S. and Dorf, B. (2012). *The startup owner's manual*. Pescadero, CA: K&S Ranch Press.

Brown, B. (2010). *The gifts of imperfection*. Center City, MN: Hazelden.

Brown, B. (2013). *Daring greatly*. London: Penguin.

Brumbaugh, R.S. (1966). 'Applied metaphysics: Truth and passing time'. *Review of Metaphysics*, **19**(4), 647–666.

CB Insights (2016). *The top 20 reasons startups fail*. Available at: www.cbinsights.com/research-reports/The-20-Reasons-Startups-Fail.pdf. Accessed on 3 January 2017.

Crawford, G.C., Aguinis, H., Lichtenstein, B., Davidsson, P. and McKelvey, B. (2015). 'Power law distributions in entrepreneurship: Implications for theory and research'. *Journal of Business Venturing*, **30**(5), 696–713.

De Bono, E. (1993). *Teach your child how to think*. London: Penguin.

Department for Business, Innovation and Skills (2015). *Business population estimates for the UK and regions 2015*. Available at: www.gov.uk/government/uploads/system/uploads/attachment_data/file/467443/bpe_2015_statistical_release.pdf. Accessed on 3 January 2017.

Dimov, D. (2010). 'Nascent entrepreneurs and venture emergence: Opportunity confidence, human capital, and early planning'. *Journal of Management Studies*, **47**(6), 1123–1153.

Dimov, D. (2011). 'Grappling with the unbearable elusiveness of entrepreneurial opportunities'. *Entrepreneurship Theory and Practice*, **35**(1), 57–81.

Dimov, D. (2016). 'Toward a design science of entrepreneurship'. In A.C. Corbett and J.A. Katz (Eds.), *Advances in entrepreneurship, firm emergence and growth*. Bingley, UK: Emerald Insight, Vol. 18, 1–31.

Dorst, K. (2011). 'The core of "design thinking" and its application'. *Design Studies*, **32**, 521–532.

Easley, D. and Kleinberg, J. (2010). *Networks, crowds, and markets: Reasoning about a highly connected world*. Cambridge, UK: Cambridge University Press.

Feld, B. (2012). *Startup communities*. Hoboken, NJ: John Wiley & Sons.

Gimeno, J., Folta, T.B., Cooper, A.C. and Woo, C.Y. (1997). 'Survival of the fittest? Entrepreneurial human capital and the persistence of underperforming firms'. *Administrative Science Quarterly*, **42**(4), 750–783.

Hart, O. and Moore, J. (1990). 'Property rights and the nature of the firm'. *Journal of Political Economy*, **98**(6), 1119–1158.

Kahneman, D. (2011). *Thinking fast and slow*. London: Allen Lane.

Kauffman, S.A. (2008). *Reinventing the sacred*. New York: Basic Books.

Kauffman Foundation (2016). *Kauffman index of startup activity 2016*. Available at: www.kauffman.org/microsites/kauffman-index/reports/startup-activity. Accessed on 3 January 2017.

Knight, F. (1921). *Risk, uncertainty and profit*. Boston, MA: Houghton Mifflin.

McMullen, J.S. and Shepherd, D.A. (2006). 'Entrepreneurial action and the role of uncertainty in the theory of the entrepreneur'. *Academy of Management Review*, **31**, 131–152.

Madrigal, A.C. (2013). 'Paul Otellini's Intel: Can the company that built the future survive it?' *The Atlantic*, 16 May 2013. Available at: www.theatlantic.com/tech nology/archive/2013/05/paul-otellinis-intel-can-the-company-that-built-the-future-survive-it/275825/. Accessed on 3 January 2017.

March, J.G. (1978). 'Bounded rationality, ambiguity, and the engineering of choice'. *The Bell Journal of Economics*, **9**(2), 587–608.

Mauboussin, M.J. (2012). *The success equation: Untangling skill and luck in business, sports, and investing*. Boston, MA: Harvard Business Review Press.

May, R.M. (1976). 'Simple mathematical models with very complicated dynamics'. *Nature*, **261**, 459–467.

Moore, G.A. (1991). *Crossing the chasm*. New York: Harper Business.

Mullins, J. and Komisar, R. (2009). *Getting to plan B: Breaking through to a better business model*. Boston, MA: Harvard Business Press.

Osterwalder, A. and Pigneur, Y. (2009). *Business model generation*. Hoboken, NJ: Wiley.

Perrow, C. (1999). *Normal accidents: Living with high-risk technologies*. New York: Basic Books.

PricewaterhouseCoopers (2016). *MoneyTree report Q4 2015/full year 2015 summary*. Available at: www.pwc.com/us/en/technology/assets/pwc-moneytree-q4-2015-summary-fullyear.pdf. Accessed on 3 January 2017.

Prigogine, I. (1997). *The end of certainty: Time, chaos, and the new laws of nature*. New York: Free Press.

Rittel, H.W.J. and Webber, M.M. (1973). 'Dilemmas in a general theory of planning'. *Policy Sciences*, **4**(2), 155–169.

Rosenzweig, P. (2007). *The halo effect*. New York: Free Press.

Ross, L. (1977). 'The intuitive psychologist and his shortcomings: Distortions in the attribution process'. In L. Berkowitz (Ed.), *Advances in experimental social psychology*. New York: Academic Press, Vol. 10, 173–220.

Salganik, M.J., Dodds, P.S. and Watts, D.J. (2006). 'Experimental study of inequality and unpredictability in an artificial cultural market'. *Science*, **311**, 854–856.

Sarasvathy, S.D. (2001). 'Causation and effectuation: Toward a theoretical shift from economic inevitability to entrepreneurial contingency'. *Academy of Management Review*, **26**(2), 243–263.

Sarasvathy, S.D., Dew, N., Read, S. and Wiltbank, R. (2008). 'Designing organizations that design environments: Lessons from entrepreneurial expertise'. *Organization Studies*, **29**(3), 331–350.

Saxenian, A.L. (1994). *Regional advantage: Culture and competition in Silicon Valley and Route 128*. Cambridge, MA: Harvard University Press.

Schon, D.A. (1983). *The reflective practitioner*. New York: Basic Books.

Wasserman, N. (2012). *The founder's dilemmas: Anticipating and avoiding the pitfalls that can sink a startup*. Princeton, NJ: Princeton University Press.

Watts, D.J. (2011). *Everything is obvious: Once you know the answer*. New York: Crown Business.

Wiltbank, R., Dew, N., Read, S. and Sarasvathy, S.D. (2006). 'What to do next? The case for non-predictive strategy'. *Strategic Management Journal*, **27**(10), 981–998.

Index

Note: Page numbers in italic indicate figures and tables.